Faith into Action

Faith into Action

**Thoughts on Selected Topics
by Daisaku Ikeda**

WORLD TRIBUNE PRESS

Published by World Tribune Press
606 Wilshire Blvd., Santa Monica, CA 90401

© 1999 Soka Gakkai

ISBN: 978-0-915678-66-2

Design by Gary Ross

20 19 18 17 16 15 14 13

CONTENTS

PART II — FAITH AND PRACTICE

PART III — LEADERSHIP

PART IV — OUR TREASURED ORGANIZATION

FOREWORD

Like ripples on a pond's surface, the wisdom of Nichiren Daishonin's Buddhism is continually expanding both in the microcosm of the individuals who practice it as well as in the macrocosm of our society and the world. And one of the greatest forces behind this spread has been the guidance and leadership of SGI President Ikeda.

Because of his example and his insights on the meaning of faith and practice in the modern age, millions of people around the world can more fully understand how to tap their own inherent power. In time for the new century, the editors of World Tribune Press have collected more than a thousand passages from the works of Mr. Ikeda and categorized them by subject for easy reference. Readers can, thanks to this new volume, at a glance find relevant quotes on topics of importance to the Buddhist practitioner and the concerned citizen of the world.

A continual theme of Mr. Ikeda's speeches, lectures and dialogues is the importance of putting our faith into practice in every sphere of our lives. Life and faith are not distinct; rather, faith finds meaning only in daily life. And Buddhist practitioners seek to apply the wisdom gained from faith to help better themselves and their world. Divided into five sections—Life; Faith and Practice; Leadership; Our Treasured Organization; and Peace, Culture and Education—this book of excerpts is sure to become a trusted guide as we make our way forward in our quest for happiness and peace. I hope that as we come to emulate the spirit contained on these pages, we will all lead lives of greater happiness, health and prosperity and help our friends and neighbors do the same.

Finally, my heartfelt thanks to President Ikeda for allowing us to compile this book and to everyone involved in its production.

Fred M. Zaitsu
SGI–USA General Director
October 2, 1999

Editor's Note

Truly vast is the scope of SGI President Ikeda's works. Speeches to members, lectures at universities, peace proposals, dialogues, poetry—the range and volume of work testify not only to his broad intellect but also to his deep concern for people as he applies the wisdom of Buddhism to every aspect of modern life. We are happy, therefore, to present this new book of excerpts grouped by subject.

Of course, because of the ocean of material from which to draw upon, we had to make some decisions, however arbitrary, about which material to include. At the same time, we wanted to be comprehensive, covering as many topics as we could practically fit into a volume of this size. We've drawn, for the most part, from Mr. Ikeda's addresses and lectures given in the 1990s, with a handful of quotes taken from the late 1980s. We've also extracted quotes from the popular books *Discussions On Youth* and *Learning From the Gosho*. When remarks on particular topics (such as "men" and "cancer") were needed, the occasional essay was excerpted. Peace proposals were also used, especially in Part V, Peace, Culture and Education.

The references at the end of each passage indicate the source of the quote. The following is an explanation of the abbreviations:

- **Date only.** Refers to the date of the speech or lecture.
- **DOY.** Refers to *Discussions On Youth*.
- **LG.** Refers to *Learning From the Gosho*.
- **PP.** Refers to the peace proposal for that year.

- **Dialogue.** Refers to a *World Tribune* series called "Dialogues" from late 1994 to early 1995.
- **WT.** Refers to *World Tribune*.
- **ST.** Refers to *Seikyo Times*.
- **LLS.** Refers to *Lectures on the "Expedient Means" and "Life Span" Chapters of the Lotus Sutra*.

In addition, within the text, citations that refer to the Lotus Sutra are abbreviated: LS, followed by the chapter and page number(s). Likewise, citations that refer to *The Major Writings of Nichiren Daishonin* are abbreviated: MW, followed by the volume and page number(s).

In the interests of clarity and brevity, the passages included here have at times been edited and/or condensed, based on a rechecking for accuracy against the original Japanese. Also, we found that most of the passages could have been grouped under more than one topic. The index thus should serve as a handy cross-reference.

Finally, we thank President Ikeda for allowing us to publish a work such as this and hope that readers will treasure it for years to come.

Life

ACTUAL PROOF

Buddhism is an earnest struggle to win. This is what the Daishonin teaches. A Buddhist must not be defeated. I hope you will maintain an alert and winning spirit in your work and daily life, taking courageous action and showing triumphant actual proof time and again. (3/8/96)

In this lifetime, to demonstrate the power of faith in the Mystic Law to others, some of you have been born into poverty so that you can show actual proof by gaining secure and comfortable lives. Some of you have been born with ill health so that you can show proof by growing strong and healthy. Irrespective of your situations, however, the light of faith in the depths of your beings will continue to shine eternally with diamond-like brilliance. (6/22/96)

Since we have taken the lead in embracing this great religion to which so much of humankind still remains oblivious, it is important that we demonstrate the value of this Buddhism by showing actual proof in our daily lives. Seeing such proof is what enables people to realize the greatness of this Buddhism, that it is something unique that they have not encountered up until now. (2/26/90)

When we speak of showing actual proof, it doesn't mean we have to try to put on a show of being any more knowledgeable or accomplished than we are. It is my hope that, in the manner that best suits your situation, you will prove the validity of this Buddhism by steadily improving in your daily life, your family, place of work and community and by polishing your character. (2/26/90)

Shijo Kingo, a person of strong faith, was at one point envied and slandered by others, earning the disfavor of his lord. But later he received a new estate from him. In modern terms, we might say that Shijo Kingo scored this victory by showing wonderful actual proof of faith at his place of work. The test of faith is winning in daily life and society, since that is where Buddhism finds expression. (4/23/96)

Science is based on tested proof or empirical evidence. You conduct a test or experiment and then observe the results. Nichiren Daishonin's Buddhism, similarly, teaches that nothing beats actual proof. In this regard, it stands alone among world religions. I hope that each year you will strive to show clear proof of victory in Buddhism and your studies. Please always remember that showing such proof is the mark of a true successor. (4/2/98)

AGING

Age is not an excuse for giving up. If you allow yourself to grow passive and draw back, it's a sign of personal defeat. There may be a retirement age at work, but there is no retirement age in life. How then could there be any retirement age in the world of faith? The Buddhist Law is eternal, extending across the three existences of past, present and future, and two of the benefits of faith are perennial youth and eternal life. (3/5/97)

∽

The finishing stages are the most important, whether for an individual or in laying the foundation of an organization. Shakyamuni taught the Lotus Sutra in the last eight years of his life. By the simplest calculation, we could say that he preached the essential teachings (the latter fourteen chapters of the Lotus Sutra), including the "Life Span of the Thus Come One" chapter, in his last four years. This chapter measures the span of the Buddha's eternal life. At the same time, it teaches that by believing in that eternal Buddha, all individuals can extend their life span. The passage "let us live out our lives" (LS16, 228) refers to this: it urges us to live long lives. (3/9/96)

∽

Life passes by in an instant. In the twinkling of an eye, we grow old. Our physical strength wanes and we begin to suffer various aches and pains. We practice Nichiren Daishonin's Buddhism so that instead of sinking into feelings of sadness, loneliness and regret, we can greet old age with inner richness and maturity, as round and complete as the ripe, golden fruit of autumn. (6/15/96)

∽

Faith exists so that we can welcome, smilingly and without regrets, an old age like a breathtaking sunset, whose dazzling rays color heaven and earth in majestic hues. (6/15/96)

∽

We find a passage in the "Former Affairs of the Bodhisattva Medicine King" chapter of the Lotus Sutra that states: "He [one who hears this sutra] will know neither old age or death" (LS23, 288). What does this mean? It does not mean we will not age or die. Rather, it refers to life-condition and life force. It means that even though we age, we will retain a youthful vitality and a spirit of eternal youth. Our lives will shine ever more brilliantly with fortune and wisdom. Buddhism focuses on the life force and life-condition required to lead lives of absolute freedom. In accord with the sutra passage, let all of us strive to live out our lives both long and vigorously. (3/9/96)

In modern society, where the highest value tends to be placed on material wealth and utility, people are often judged on whether they are useful. This would not be the case in a civilization that treasures human maturity and depth of wisdom. If there is value in the young shoots of spring and the light of summer, then there must also be value in the mature trees of autumn and the grand sunsets of winter. (LG, p. 187)

There is no retirement age in faith. Sincere faith never ages. Those who exert themselves for the sake of the Law are ever young. Our heart is what matters most. Let us strive to the end of our days for kosen-rufu. (3/8/98)

For those who practice Buddhism, old age is a time of unsurpassed fulfillment when we put the finishing touches on the golden journal of our lives and attain Buddhahood; days of mission when we show actual proof and relate to others the wonder of life and power of the spirit we have experienced. (LG, p. 187)

APPRECIATION

Buddhism is concerned with the essential nature of humanity. Buddhism is not found somewhere separate from such beautiful expressions of humanity as appreciation toward one's mother or courtesy to others. As Nichiren Daishonin teaches in the Gosho, "behavior as a human being" that perfectly accords with reason is what constitutes the heart of Buddhism. Therefore, our world of faith must be a gathering that is full of affection and heartfelt consideration. (2/22/90)

The Gohonzon will never demand that you chant to it. An attitude of appreciation in being able to chant to the Gohonzon is the heart of faith. The more you exert yourselves in faith in doing gongyo and chanting daimoku, the more you stand to gain. (DOY 2, ch. 19)

To "enjoy what there is to enjoy" means to cause the "mystic lotus of the heart" (*Gosho Zenshu*, p. 978) to blossom brightly with a sense of appreciation and joy. Someone who can find joy, who can feel appreciation, experiences a snowballing exhilaration and joy in life. Such is the heart's function. (LG, p. 245)

Appreciation is what makes people truly human. The Japanese word for *thankful* originally indicated a rare or unusual condition and later came to denote a sense of joyful appreciation for an uncommon occurrence. Having a spirit of appreciation for someone from whose actions we benefit, a sense that "this is the rarest and noblest thing," produces in our hearts a feeling of pride and self-esteem: "I am worthy of receiving such goodness." It provides us with spiritual support to go on living. (LG, p. 28)

ATTITUDE

I want you to understand the subtle workings of the mind. How you orient your mind, the kind of attitude you take, greatly influences both you and your environment. The Buddhist principle of 3,000 realms in a single moment of life completely elucidates the true aspect of life's inner workings. Through the power of strong inner resolve, we can transform ourselves, those around us and the land in which we live. (3/24/97)

It is not a question of your environment, those around you, or what the organization or leaders may be like. To be swayed by such externals is pointless. It all comes down to one person: you. What matters is that you become a brilliant beacon, shining with joy and happiness, and live your life with confidence and courage. If you shine with radiant light, there can be no darkness in your life. (4/23/96)

Resolve to be the sun. This is the first thing you must do. As long as you are the sun, no matter what problems you may be facing now, the dawn will always break, fine weather will always return, and spring will never fail to arrive. (DOY 1, ch. 2)

In Buddhism, nothing happens by chance. Everything has meaning. Please be convinced that you already possess every treasure. It's vital to recognize that no matter how difficult your situation may be you are alive now. There is no treasure more precious than life itself. Furthermore, you are still young and blessed with a youthful spirit, the greatest treasure in the universe. Please do not destroy or harm that treasure by giving way to feelings of despair. (DOY 1, ch. 2)

The course of our lives is determined by how we react— what we decide and what we do—at the darkest of times. The nature of that response determines a person's true worth and greatness. (5/3/96)

The purpose of life is to be happy. We should not be pessimistic. Let us live always with optimism—joyful, strong and bright. That is why we practice the Daishonin's Buddhism. (6/9/96)

One thing is certain: The power of belief, the power of thought, will move reality in the direction of our belief. If you really believe you can do something, you can. That is a fact. (3/9/93)

We often hear people say they aren't capable. But this is a defeatist attitude. If you feel you aren't capable, then tap into the great reservoir of potential inside you. Since we embrace the Daishonin's Buddhism, we have recourse to daimoku. If we chant daimoku to the Gohonzon, we can bring forth all the ability and strength we will ever need. (7/19/96)

The moment you start grumbling, complaining or harboring ill feelings toward your fellow members, you immediately forfeit a substantial portion of all the good fortune you have worked so hard to attain. Therefore, if you're practicing faith, you stand to gain far more when you do so willingly, joyously and with a sense of gratitude. (1/31/93)

Everything depends on what is in our hearts. Heartfelt prayers will definitely be answered. If we decide that something is impossible, then, consistent with our minds thinking so, even possible things will become impossible. On the other hand, if we have the confidence that we can definitely do something, we are one step closer to achieving it. (LG, p. 129)

Just because we practice the Daishonin's Buddhism doesn't make us in any way special. Essentially we are in no way different from other people except for the fact that we base ourselves on daimoku, that is, chanting to the Gohonzon. There is no such thing as a special kind of human being. To assume an elitist air is the behavior of fanatics. We have no room for such people in the SGI. (9/26/93)

When you do gongyo joyfully and carry out activities with the determination to accumulate more good fortune in your life, the heavenly deities will be delighted and will valiantly perform their duty. If you must take some action anyway, it is to your advantage that you do so spontaneously, with a feeling of joy. (2/27/90)

In accordance with the principle of 3,000 realms in a single moment of life, pessimistic thoughts or feelings take form, just as they are, in reality, producing negative results. People who have negative thoughts create effects for themselves that perfectly match their thinking. So it is important to be optimistic.

There is no such thing as pessimism in Buddhism. The Lotus Sutra gives us the key that enables us to possess great confidence and burn with hope, even amid circumstances that appear dire. Nichiren Daishonin proved this with his life. (LG, p. 129)

∽

People tend to become envious over the slightest thing, which is, perhaps, human nature. They may try to undercut someone they envy and delight at the person's misfortune. We must not be defeated by this pitiful tendency. To allow ourselves to become caught up in or swayed by whirlpools of emotion, going from elation one moment to dejection the next, is pointless. (LG, p. 239)

∽

If you practice faith yet have an attitude of complaint, you will destroy your good fortune in direct proportion. Those who are full of complaint are not respected by others. From both Buddhist and secular perspectives, their behavior does not befit a wise or worthy person. (1/31/93)

∽

Whether we regard difficulties in life as misfortunes or whether we view them as good fortune depends entirely on how much we have forged our inner determination. It all depends on our attitude, our inner state of life. With a dauntless spirit, we can lead a cheerful and thoroughly enjoyable life. We can develop a "self" of such fortitude that we look forward to life's trials and tribulations with a sense of profound elation and joy: "Come on obstacles! I've been expecting you! This is the chance that I've been waiting for!" (5/21/95)

∽

The mentality of getting others to do the hard work while one sits back and takes it easy is bureaucracy at its worst; it is not faith. The spirit of taking on the hard work oneself — that is faith, that is humanism. (8/27/97)

One of my favorite Argentine poets, the great educator Almafuerte (1854–1917) wrote: "To the weak, difficulty is a closed door. To the strong, however, it is a door waiting to be opened." Difficulties impede the progress of those who are weak. For the strong, however, they are opportunities to open wide the doors to a bright future. Everything is determined by our attitude, by our resolve. Our heart is what matters most. (3/18/98)

You can forge the path to a fulfilling and enjoyable life if you have the depth of faith to regard everything as a source for creating happiness and value. Conversely, if you see everything only in a negative or pessimistic light, your life will gradually but inevitably be plunged into darkness. Buddhism teaches the subtle principle of *ichinen* and the power of faith. (2/12/90)

We have both a weak self and a strong self; the two are completely different. If we allow our weak side to dominate, we will be defeated. The thought "I am still young and have a lot of time, so I can relax and take life easy" is a function of weakness. (3/24/97)

The Daishonin refers to examples and passages from the scriptures that are appropriate for the recipients to change their hearts, strengthen their determinations and give them

confidence and conviction. He radiates hope and encouragement, like the sun. This is because he fully understood that
changing one's mental attitude changes everything. (3/9/93)

Viewing events and situations in a positive light is important.
The strength, wisdom and cheerfulness that accompany such
an attitude lead to happiness. To regard everything in a positive light or with a spirit of goodwill, however, does not mean
being foolishly gullible and allowing people to take advantage
of our good nature. It means having the wisdom and perception to move things in a positive direction by seeing things in
their best light while all the time keeping our eyes firmly fo-
cused on reality. (6/23/96)

The brilliance of true humanity lies in surmounting feelings
of envy with the resolute attitude "I'll create an even more
wonderful life for myself." If you are jealous of others, you will
not advance; you will only become miserable. Please do not
be defeated or consumed by such emotions. (DOY 1, ch. 6)

BROAD-MINDEDNESS

If you always have a shallow perspective and pay attention only
to trivial things, you are sure to get bogged down in petty concerns and will not be able to move forward. Even relatively minor hurdles or problems will seem insurmountable. But if you
look at life from a broad viewpoint, you will naturally spot the
solution for any problem you confront. This is true when we
consider our personal problems as well as those of society and
even the future of the entire world. (DOY 2, ch. 14)

Those who are tolerant and broad-minded make people feel comfortable and at ease. Narrow, intolerant people who go around berating others for the slightest thing, or who make a great commotion each time some problem arises, just exhaust everyone and inspire fear. Leaders must not intimidate or exhaust others. They must be tolerant and have a warm approachability that makes people feel relaxed and comfortable. Not only are those who possess a heart as wide as the ocean happy themselves, but those around them are happy, too. (6/23/96)

Pioneers in the movement for human rights are bound to face persecution from entrenched authorities and the powers that be. This is a historical constant; it is inescapable. All victories for human rights have been won as the fruit of arduous struggles. So it is necessary to always view things from a long-range perspective. With this in mind, one becomes able to perceive the essence of the matter and to see the broad path to victory that lies ahead. (2/5/91)

The heart of one person moves another's. If your heart is closed, then the doors to other people's hearts will also shut tight. On the other hand, someone who turns all those around him or her into allies, bathing them in the sunlight of spring, as it were, will be treasured by all. A Buddhist way of life must embody such clear and natural reasoning. The Buddha transmits the heart's sunlight universally to all beings. (LG, p. 148)

Even when we strive to treat everyone with love and compassion, since we are ordinary people, it is only natural that we will have likes and dislikes. There is no need for us to struggle to make ourselves fond of people we find disagreeable. In our work as emissaries of the Buddha, however, we must not let our thoughts or actions be colored by discrimination or favoritism. (LG, p. 148)

It's much more valuable to look for the strengths in others. You gain nothing by criticizing people's imperfections. To develop a bigger heart, please try chanting, even a little at a time, for the happiness of your friends. Gradually, you will cultivate tolerance and broad-mindedness. (DOY 1, ch. 10)

CHALLENGE

Life is a process of ongoing challenge. Those who lead lives of boundless challenge realize boundless growth. In a time of tumultuous change, what people need most is vitality to challenge their circumstances and the wisdom to open the treasure house of knowledge, to ceaselessly strive to create new value. (3/21/96)

Life is a struggle. So, too, are Buddhism and kosen-rufu. If young people, in particular, are reluctant to strive hard and exert themselves, they will be unable to build strong characters. As Shakespeare said, "Plenty and peace breeds cowards; hardness ever / Of hardiness is mother." In other words, hardship is the source of strength and fortitude. (Dialogue 4)

What is the treasure of youth? It is struggle; it is hard work. Unless you struggle, you cannot become truly strong. Those who work hard during their youth will have nothing to fear when the time comes to put the finishing touches on their lives. They will possess a great state of life that towers strong and unshakable. In Buddhism, we call this the state of Buddhahood, which nothing can undermine or destroy. It is a state of mind enjoyed by invincible champions of life. (10/25/96)

Chant abundant daimoku and strive in your personal growth as you do so. Faith means setting goals, working toward them and striving to realize each one. If we view each goal or challenge as a mountain, faith is a process whereby we grow with each mountain climbed. (DOY 2, ch. 19)

Rather than sitting around idly and rusting, we must act, give of ourselves and contribute something to the world. The French scholar Robert Arnauld (1588–1674) declared, "Have we not all eternity to rest in?" He asks, why do you seek to rest while you are still alive? These are venerable words indeed. When young people make truly dedicated efforts, almost punishing themselves, their true brilliance will shine forth. (7/19/96)

The functions of both the devil and the Buddha exist within our lives. Ultimately, our battle is with ourselves. Whether in our Buddhist practice, in activities in society, in historic, political or economic developments, everything essentially boils down to a struggle between positive and negative forces. (3/24/97)

Our lives are ruled by impermanence. But simply realizing that changes nothing. There is no value in bleak pessimism. The challenge is how to create something of enduring value within the context of our impermanent lives. The Lotus Sutra teaches us how to do this. (3/29/96)

It's foolish to be obsessed with past failures. It's just as foolish to be self-satisfied with one's small achievements. Buddhism teaches that the present and the future are what are important, not the past. Buddhism teaches us a spirit of unceasing challenge to win over the present and advance toward the future. Those who neglect this spirit of continual striving steer their lives in a ruinous direction. (1/26/96)

CHEERFULNESS

Emerson writes: "And so of cheerfulness, or a good temper, the more it is spent, the more of it remains." Cheerfulness is not the same as frivolousness. Cheerfulness is born of a fighting spirit. Frivolousness is the reverse side of cowardly escape. Emerson also said that "power dwells with cheerfulness; hope puts us in a working mood." Without cheerfulness there is no strength. Let us strive to advance still more brightly and cheerfully. (1/6/96)

Those who are always wearing long, gloomy expressions whenever you meet them, who have lost the ability to rejoice and feel genuine delight or wonder, live a dark, cheerless existence. On the other hand, those who possess good cheer can hear even a scolding by a loved one, such as a spouse or partner, as sweet music to their ears; or they can greet a child's poor report card as a sign that there is great potential for improvement in the future. Viewing events and situations in this kind of positive light is important. The strength, wisdom and cheerfulness that accompany such an attitude lead to happiness. (6/23/96)

A victor is one whose life shines with faith. Emerson, one of the favorite writers of my youth, once said, "That which befits us...is cheerfulness and courage, and the endeavor to realize our aspirations." To advance toward our dreams cheerfully, to courageously work toward achieving them—this is what gives sublime meaning and value to our lives. (5/26/98)

The present, as I am sure you all sense, is an age pervaded by great weariness and apathy. I would like you to be aware that the power and energy to serve humanity in such an enervated age can only be born of a vigorous, indomitable, noble will. Though the times may be rife with petty human conflicts, a pervading sense of hopelessness and all manner of turbulent storms, I hope that all of you will forge ahead boldly, with unflagging good cheer. (4/2/96)

COMPASSION

It is important for each person to embark on a journey in search of the truth. The truth, however, actually lies in compassionate actions to assist the weak or those enduring hardship and suffering. It is not to be found in highbrow, intellectual knowledge. (4/6/98)

To possess both wisdom and compassion is the heart of our human revolution. If you have wisdom alone and lack compassion, it will be a cold, perverse wisdom. If you have compassion alone and lack wisdom, you cannot give happiness to others. You are even likely to lead them in the wrong direction. You also won't be able to achieve your own happiness. (2/5/93)

~

Without courage we cannot be compassionate. Courage and compassion are inseparable, like the two sides of a coin. Faith is the wellspring of courage. The Daishonin says, "Nichiren's disciples cannot accomplish anything if they are cowardly" (MW-1, 128). A cowardly person cannot realize victory in life. Unless we have the courage to really dedicate our lives to kosen-rufu, we cannot construct true happiness for ourselves or others. (2/3/98)

~

Compassion is the very soul of Buddhism. To pray for others, making their problems and anguish our own; to embrace those who are suffering, becoming their greatest ally; to continue giving them our support and encouragement until they become truly happy—it is in such humanistic actions that the Daishonin's Buddhism lives and breathes. (1/27/93)

~

Concerned about the illness of Toki Jonin's wife, Nichiren Daishonin wrote the following encouragement: "I think of your wife's illness as if it were my own, and am praying to heaven day and night for her recovery" (*Gosho Zenshu*, p. 978). In this passage we can sense the Daishonin's infinitely profound compassion. (1/27/93)

~

The Daishonin was at once dauntlessly strong toward arrogant authorities and infinitely kind toward people of sincerity.

These are both manifestations of his compassion. This sums up Nichiren Daishonin's sublime humanity. (LG, p. 15)

As Buddhists, we need to be sensitive to other people's situations, to put out the "antennas of the heart," as it were. Such concern and sensitivity, which the Daishonin teaches by his own example, are essential parts of the makeup of a Buddhist. (LG, p. 33)

A strong person is gentle. "Birds cry, but never shed tears. I, Nichiren, do not cry, but my tears flow ceaselessly" (MW-1, 94). Nichiren Daishonin wrote these famous words while in exile on Sado Island. He had great, abounding compassion. He was the perfect embodiment of profound feeling and towering wisdom. (LG, p. 154)

The Japanese word for *compassion* includes the meaning of suffering together or crying out in sympathy with others. The Buddha, first of all, shares others' sufferings. (LG, p. 155)

At its root, compassion is the spirit to suffer alongside and pray with those who are suffering. The Daishonin possessed such a spirit. He joined Ueno-ama Gozen, the mother of Nanjo Tokimitsu (Lord Ueno), in her grief and tears when her youngest son, Shichiro Goro, died at the tender age of 16. He continued to offer her encouragement until she regained the will to go on living. (LG, p. 158)

DEATH

President Toda once said: "The last years of one's life are the most important. If you are happy during the last years of your life, your life has been a happy one. Whether it be the last three years, seven years, or ten years, Buddhism guarantees that those who practice will approach death in a state of supreme happiness." (3/9/96)

It is at the moment of death that one's past causes show most plainly in one's appearance. At that time there is no way to conceal the truth of your soul. We carry out our Buddhist practice now so that we will not have to experience any regret or torment on our deathbeds. (2/27/90)

When winter arrives, trees and other plants temporarily lose their leaves. But those plants and trees possess the life to send forth new green shoots when spring comes. Human death is like that, but we possess a life force that leads us to a new life—to a new mission—immediately and without pain. (2/20/90)

Death is a certainty. Therefore, it's not whether our lives are long or short but whether, while alive, we form a connection with the Mystic Law—the eternal elixir for all life's ills. That, in retrospect, determines whether we have led the best possible lives. By virtue of our having formed such a connection, we will again quickly return to the stage of kosen-rufu. The important thing is that surviving family and friends live with dignity and realize great happiness based on this conviction. Their happiness shows that they have conquered the hindrance of death and eloquently attests to the deceased's attainment of Buddhahood. (LG, p. 171)

Since we are human, we will as a matter of course undergo the four sufferings—birth, aging, sickness and death. The important thing is that we withstand the onslaught of these sufferings and overcome them with true nobility. (LG, p. 173)

What is death? What becomes of us after we die? Failing to pursue these questions is like spending our student years without considering what to do after graduating. Without coming to terms with death, we cannot establish a strong direction in life. Pursuing this issue brings real stability and depth to our lives. (LG, p. 180)

Everyone has to face death one day. At that time, those who walk the path of the Mystic Law will make their way serenely to Eagle Peak aboard the great white ox cart described in the Lotus Sutra. They will merge with the universal Buddhahood. Even the most sophisticated space rocket cannot compare to the great white ox cart. Riding on this wondrous vehicle of the Law, we soar freely toward the destination where our next mission awaits. As the Lotus Sutra indicates when it says those who uphold the Law "freely choose where they will be born" (LS10, 163), we can be reborn wherever and in whatever form we desire. (6/15/96)

If we attain the state of Buddhahood in this lifetime, that state will forever pervade our lives. Throughout the cycle of birth and death, in each new lifetime, we will be endowed with good health, wealth and intelligence along with a supportive and comfortable environment, leading a life that overflows with good fortune. Each of us will also possess a unique mission and be born in an appropriate form to fulfill it. (6/15/96)

~

To die happily is extremely difficult. And since death is the final settlement of accounts for one's life, that is when our true self comes to the fore. We practice faith to live happily and to die happily. One who has faith in the Mystic Law will not die unhappily. (9/26/96)

~

Our existence in this world can be likened to a dream. The issue of greatest importance and eternal relevance is how we face death, the inescapable destiny of all living beings. For in the face of death, external factors such as social status or position in the organization count for naught. Everything then depends on one's faith, one's true state of life. (9/26/96)

~

Death will come to each of us some day. We can die having fought hard for our beliefs and convictions, or we can die having failed to do so. Since the reality of death is the same in either case, isn't it far better that we set out on our journey toward the next existence in high spirits, with a bright smile on our faces, knowing that in everything we did, we did the very best we could, thrilling with the sense that "That was truly an interesting life"? (8/27/97)

~

The state of mind with which we meet death will greatly influence the course of our lives over eternity. If one is unconcerned by how one dies, or if one dismisses any connection between this existence and the next, then there probably isn't any need to practice the Daishonin's Buddhism. But the truth is that life is eternal, that our existence continues even after we die. Moreover, during the latent stage of death before rebirth, we cannot change the essence of our lives, we cannot carry out a Buddhist practice. Only while we are alive as human beings can we practice Buddhism. (3/24/97)

DIVERSITY

I hope you will skillfully use diversity, transcending differences, harmonizing the various aspects of diversity, and moving everything in the direction of happiness and security. In this way, you can create the values of beauty, benefit and goodness. (8/7/92)

An example of diversity is the changing colors of a mountain as shadows subtly shift in hue and range depending on the season and time of day. Talented artists can capture the supreme beauty of the mountain's fleeting changes of expression in their mind's eye and create masterpieces. Those who enjoy differences and discover the greatest beauty and value in them are masters in life. This is a life of wisdom based upon Nichiren Daishonin's Buddhism. (8/7/92)

Buddhism expounds that all kinds of people exist in the realm of living beings (*shujo seken*), or society. *Seken* indicates differences, which implies diversity. There are all kinds of people. That is good. It would be boring if people were all the same. The United States is the epitome of such diversity. It has the potential to become an ideal nation. (8/7/92)

Life is diverse. Human beings are diverse. That is the natural way of things. The opposite of diversity is standardization, totalitarianism, dictatorship or despotism. For instance, the eyes, nose, mouth, hands and legs all have their own diverse functions, yet each plays an important role. One is not superior or inferior to the other. When this diversity is harnessed into a harmonious whole, the different parts function as part of an organic entity, allowing the whole to become a wonderful, functioning, creative organism. (8/7/92)

The purpose of Buddhism is to bring out the Buddha nature that all people inherently possess, to awaken people to it and enable them to attain Buddhahood. Moreover, the Lotus Sutra does not allow for any discrimination; all people are equally entitled to salvation. Thus, to deny equality is to deny the Lotus Sutra. (9/23/91)

In accordance with the principle of "cherry, plum, peach and damson blossoms" (a metaphor for each person's uniqueness), let us strive even harder to realize the full blossoming of springtime, the dawning of a renaissance of Buddhism, which aims for the blossoming of each person's individuality. In every society, the period of winter must be brought to an end. (1/16/91)

The Lotus Sutra embodies a philosophy that most highly respects, fosters and harmonizes human diversity. The Mystic Law is the source that enables us to manifest our unique brilliance against a backdrop of mutual understanding and appreciation of one another's differences; to create a lush flower garden of "cherry, plum, peach and damson blossoms." (6/15/96)

In the multitude of human personalities, we see the Buddhist principle of cherry, plum, peach and damson blossom at work. Just as each blossom is beautiful in its own way, each person is endowed with special qualities. Being introverted doesn't make someone incapable, just as being quick-tempered doesn't make a person useless. The fundamental aim of Buddhism is to live in a way that is true to ourselves. (DOY 1, ch. 10)

Only through learning can we open the spiritual windows of humanity, releasing people from the confines of ethnic or other group-based worldviews. Ethnic identity is deeply rooted in the human unconscious, and it is crucial that it be tempered through unremitting educational efforts that encourage a more open and universal sense of humanity. (1996 PP)

Intercultural contacts on levels that probe and bring into question unique cultural practices deeply rooted in people's daily lives can easily evoke reactions of aversion or even hostility. Never is a deep, inner-generated spirit of restraint and self-control so required of people as when they are confronted with the confusion and tensions brought about by a collision of cultures. True partnership cannot be attained unless the effort to create it is based on mutual self-control at this inner, spiritual level. (3/27/91)

EFFORT

We must make steady and persistent efforts that are firmly grounded in daily life. If we travel in the orbit of "faith equals daily life," all our prayers will definitely be answered. We can then lead a life in which all our desires are fulfilled. (6/5/96)

Your environment does not matter. Everything starts with you. You must forge yourself through your own efforts. I urge each of you to create something, start something and make a success of something. That is the essence of human existence, the challenge of youth. Herein lies a wonderful way of life, always aiming for the future. (7/19/96)

I call to each of you: Strive for prosperity! Strive for development! Strive for victory! Life is about striving all out to achieve our aims. It is about hard work and effort. Regardless of how smart you may be, intelligence alone cannot guarantee your future. (3/18/98)

It all comes down to hard work, to tenacious efforts. You cannot become a person of the highest caliber if you have a casual, easygoing attitude, thinking things will somehow just fall into place. Beethoven's motto was "No day without a line." Every day, without fail, he wrote music. He would not let even a single day pass without working assiduously. He had to leave behind something for posterity! This was the spirit of Beethoven, a giant of art. (2/24/96)

The road we walk is not level. We must climb a great mountain, a task that invariably requires painful effort. However, in the world of Buddhism, no effort is wasted or in vain. All causes that you make will be engraved in the depths of your life; they are passages in the golden diary of your eternal existence. (2/14/90)

Should all our prayers be answered without our having to make any effort, we would grow lazy. Should all our desires be achieved without our ever having to experience suffering or hardship, we would not be able to understand the pain and struggles of others, and our compassion would gradually wane. (6/5/96)

Certainly there will be times when you wish you had more spending money, more time to sleep and more time for fun and recreation. You may feel restricted now, but you should consider your current situation as the perfect set of circumstances for your growth. Within the restrictions that define your present existence, the only thing to do is to discipline yourself and head in the direction of growth and self-improvement. In the process of exerting yourself in such endeavors, you will without a doubt build and strengthen your character. (4/27/96)

"All right, let's get to work again!" This is the spirit of people of genuine substance. Those who avoid hard work or neglect the things they have to do, who just while away their time, eating, sleeping, playing, watching television—such individuals will never experience true happiness, satisfaction or joy. (7/16/98)

Shakyamuni proclaims, "People who are vigilant do not die; people who are negligent are as if dead." This is definitely true. Unremitting diligence in our Buddhist practice—brave and vigorous exertion—infuses our lives with the great life force of the eternal Buddha. In contrast, people who try to get by in life through cunning and deception enact a living death. (1/8/98)

The ultimate essence of Nichiren Daishonin's Buddhism lies in living through to the very end, pressing ever forward, courageously taking on each new challenge we encounter and never giving up. Constructing the eternal glory of the state of Buddhahood within our own lives is the purpose of our Buddhist practice in this lifetime. Hence the Daishonin's constant urging that we make tenacious efforts in the present. (4/22/96)

ENVIRONMENT

Sometimes, incidents happen that may cause us to have doubts and make us feel, "Why did this kind of thing have to happen again?" or "This is really discouraging." But allowing ourselves to be swayed by our environment only makes those around us gloomy and despondent as well. It benefits no one. This is the very time that we must summon the faith to turn poison into medicine. Through our inner determination based on faith, we can transform suffering into joy, problems into happiness, negative karma into benefit. We can change everything into a sparkling world of eternal happiness. (2/27/92)

People tend to overlook the value and worthiness of those things that are close at hand. In Buddhism, however, the reality

of the present time and the place where we live is of the utmost importance. (9/27/91)

The place where we are right now is what matters. This is all
the more true for us who embrace the Mystic Law. Buddhism
teaches that we can transform wherever we are into the Land
of Eternally Tranquil Light. (3/8/96)

In a passage of the "Record of the Orally Transmitted
Teachings," the Daishonin observes, "When you bow to a
mirror, the reflected image bows back" (*Gosho Zenshu*,
p. 769). People who respect others are respected by others
in turn. Those who are unstinting in their compassion and
concern for others are also protected and supported by others. Our environment is essentially a reflection of ourselves.
(6/10/96)

FAITH EQUALS DAILY LIFE

Faith manifests itself in daily life. Daily life, in turn, is the
stage upon which we show proof of faith. True human victory and happiness are attained through the earnest and steady
day-to-day efforts we make. The pattern of our lives, like that
of the sun, may seem monotonous and routine, but there is
nothing more profound than our daily endeavors. Achieving
brilliant victory in our daily lives is what being victorious in
faith is all about. (9/26/93)

One who takes good care of his or her job, daily life and
family is a person of deep and genuine faith. Activities are

intended to be carried out in the spare time that you have from work and family. (2/25/90)

Please steadily advance along the fundamental path of "faith manifests itself in daily life," living in the way that best suits you. Just as the sun rises every day, if you persistently advance based on the Mystic Law, the absolute Law of the universe, you can definitely lead a life in which all desires are fulfilled, a life of which you cannot now even conceive. Please be convinced that you are now leading the most certain and valuable life. (2/26/90)

We have been born, and life is made for living. It is important that we strive to live on tenaciously to the very end, no matter what happens. Faith in the Mystic Law supplies us with the immense life force we need to live strongly and confidently each day so that we can overcome the various sufferings and hardships we encounter. (6/19/96)

Faith and daily life, faith and work—these are not separate things. They are one and the same. To think of them as separate—that faith is faith and work is work—is theoretical faith. Based on the recognition that work and faith are one and the same, we should put 100 percent of our energy into our jobs and 100 percent into our faith, too. When we resolve to do this, we enter the path of victory in life. Faith means to show irrefutable proof of victory amid the realities of society and in our own daily lives. (10/6/95)

When we plant the seed of happiness that is faith and carefully tend its growth, it will produce fruit without fail. We have to keep in mind, however, that we cannot plant a seed today and expect it to bear fruit tomorrow. That's not reasonable and Buddhism is reason. If we persevere in the practice of "faith equals daily life" in accord with reason, then our prayers will definitely be answered. This is Nichiren Daishonin's promise to us. And his words are true beyond any doubt. (6/9/96)

FAMILY

Outward appearance is not important. What counts is what is inside our hearts. Are there heart-to-heart bonds? Some families may always be together physically but are estranged at heart. Some families can only get together for brief periods but manage to enjoy concentrated and lively heart-to-heart communication whenever they do meet. Families that share bonds of closeness based on day-to-day efforts are families in which the members feel comfortable and at ease with one another no matter where they are or what they're doing. (2/3/93)

We SGI members devote ourselves to serving the Law, to serving humanity. Ours is not an egocentric life. That is why we are busier than others and perhaps don't have as much opportunity for relaxation with our families. Nevertheless, we continue to devote ourselves to others. Ours is the most noble way of life. We must make sure our children understand and respect our beliefs, our way of life and our dedication. We must make conscious efforts to verbalize and communicate our thoughts and feelings to them. Finding the wisdom for this task is an expression of our faith. (2/3/93)

The family is a unit where all joys and sorrows are shared among its members. As a result, sadness is more than halved and happiness more than doubled. (2/25/90)

Our society and our schools may operate on a cold, unemotional principle of competition, judging and selecting people by their abilities and appearances. That is precisely why it is important for the family to be a fair and equitable place where each member is valued for being a unique individual. (2/3/93)

Neither orders, authority nor threats can unite a family. It is love, harmony and consideration that bind its members to one another. In a family, there is no particular need for a hero. What is needed is a strong father who can protect everyone and a mother who is impartial, fair and kind. (2/25/90)

I imagine that some of you have family members who are not yet practicing Nichiren Daishonin's Buddhism. There is no need to be impatient about or to agonize over this. Whether people take faith has to do with their mystic connection with Buddhism, a connection that takes a variety of forms. Most important is the presence of one person who is practicing. One person's attainment of Buddhahood brings happiness to all family members and relatives and those around him or her. When a single sun rises, the whole earth is illuminated. (2/24/96)

GOALS

When you devote your life to achieving your goal, you will not be bothered by shallow criticism. In fact, nothing important can be accomplished if you allow yourself to be swayed by some trifling matter, always looking over your shoulder and wondering what others are saying or thinking. The key to achievement is to move forward along your chosen path with deep determination. (2/17/96)

There is a saying that people will not exceed their dreams. That is why you should have big dreams. But you must recognize that dreams are dreams and reality is reality. It's natural, therefore, that to achieve big dreams, you must view your situation realistically and work with your entire being to ensure that they come true. (DOY 1, ch. 8)

I would like you to be people of solid character who possess rich common sense. To become people of magnificent character, upstanding citizens in society, loved and respected members of your families—this is the true goal of Buddhist practitioners. (9/26/93)

People generally tend to see or stress only results. But a person of action gives thought and consideration to the process that leads to success. The attainment of one's goal is none other than a tale of unspeakable trials. (2/16/90)

The greater the struggle, the more enriching the experience. That said, if you immediately set out to climb a high peak without preparation, the challenge could be beyond you. You may be forced to abandon your ascent, losing your way or even suffering altitude sickness! It might be better to first attempt a goal suited to your level. (DOY 2, ch. 13)

We must live our lives wisely and thoughtfully. Many people tend to give up on the way to reaching their goal, thinking they've hit a dead end. Though it may be long and difficult, however, there is always another route to follow to the same destination. (DOY 2, ch. 16)

The resolve to accomplish your goals is what counts. If you earnestly put your mind to something, your brain, your body, your environment—everything—will start working toward achieving that goal. (4/2/96)

Buddhism teaches us that the individual writes and performs the script for his or her own life. Neither chance nor a divine being writes the script for us. We write it, and we are the actors who play it. This is an extremely positive philosophy, inherent in the teaching of 3,000 realms in a single moment of life. You are the author and the hero. To perform your play well, it is important to pound the script into your head so thoroughly that you can see it vividly before your eyes. You may need to rehearse in your mind. Sometimes it helps to write down your goals, copying them over and over until they are inscribed in your heart. (3/9/93)

This lifetime will never come again; it is precious and irreplaceable. To live without regret, it is crucial for us to have a concrete purpose and continually set goals and challenges for ourselves. It is equally important that we keep moving toward specific targets steadily and tenaciously, one step at a time. (2/21/98)

HAPPINESS

Life proceeds along a path, though the path is invisible. There is definitely a path for human beings that leads to absolute happiness—and that path is the road of the Mystic Law. If we continue to advance along this road without abandoning our faith, we will definitely come to savor a state of life in which all our desires are fulfilled both spiritually and materially. (6/15/96)

From the standpoint of the eternity of our lives, because we embrace the Mystic Law everything is moving in a positive direction, everything contributes to our happiness and our attainment of Buddhahood. We need to have confidence in the Mystic Law. We mustn't be swayed by immediate circumstances or allow them to cloud our faith. (5/19/97)

Happiness is not something that someone else, like a lover, can give to us. We have to achieve it for ourselves. And the only way to do so is by developing our character and capacity as human beings by fully maximizing our potential. If we sacrifice our growth and talent for love, we absolutely will not find happiness. True happiness is obtained through fully realizing our potential. (DOY 1, ch. 7)

Why are human beings born? This question has posed a great challenge. President Toda lucidly set forward his conclusion. Namely, that this world is a place for people to "enjoy themselves at ease." We were born here to thoroughly savor the joys of life. Faith in the Daishonin's Buddhism is what enables us to bring forth the great life force we need to lead such an existence. (3/3/96)

There is a saying, "A small heart gets used to misery and becomes docile, while a great heart towers above misfortune."
True happiness is not the absence of suffering; you cannot
have day after day of clear skies. True happiness lies in building a self that stands dignified and indomitable like a great
palace—on all days, even when it is raining, snowing or
stormy. (LG, p. 241)

To experience the "joy derived from the Law" means to fully savor the unchanging Mystic Law and the power and wisdom that derive from it. In contrast to this joy, there is the
"joy derived from desires"—the enjoyment that comes from
fulfilling desires. While it might seem like genuine happiness,
such joy is only temporary and superficial. It does not arise
from the depths of our lives and will soon give way to unhappiness and dissatisfaction. Faith enables us to receive the
eternal joy derived from the Law. So let us engrave in our
hearts this point: We ourselves receive this joy. Because we receive it ourselves, our happiness does not depend on others.
No one else can make us happy. Only by our own efforts can
we become happy. (LG, p. 237)

Our lives are infinitely precious. Not to attain a state of absolute happiness in this lifetime is a great loss. Our Buddhist
practice exists so that we can attain indestructible happiness.
We must fight to the fullest right now, not at some time in
the future. (1/30/95)

To be filled each day with a rewarding sense of exhilaration
and purpose, a sense of tasks accomplished and deep fulfillment—people who feel this way are happy. Those who have
this sense of satisfaction even if they are extremely busy are

much happier than those who have free time on their hands but feel empty inside. (6/23/96)

Happiness does not lie in outward appearances or vanity. Rather it is a matter of what you yourself feel inside; it is a deep, answering response in your life. (6/26/96)

What is the purpose of life? It is happiness. But there are two kinds of happiness: relative and absolute. Relative happiness comes in a wide variety of forms. The purpose of Buddhism is to attain Buddhahood. In modern terms, this could be explained as realizing absolute happiness—a state of happiness that can never be destroyed or defeated. (2/27/90)

The Daishonin teaches the meaning of true happiness and the true purpose of life. Fame and momentary glories are no more than illusions. True happiness lies in cultivating the great state of Buddhahood within one's life. This is life's true purpose. By chanting daimoku, we can change all of our sufferings into ingredients for attaining a Buddha's lofty state of life. (1/6/96)

Buddhism is about bringing happiness, joy and fulfillment to all. It enables us not only to become happy ourselves but to make causes for the enlightenment of our ancestors seven-plus generations back and for the happiness and prosperity of our children, grandchildren and descendants throughout future generations. This is the great benefit of Buddhism. (3/13/98)

Those who have experienced great suffering must win in life and become happy. If you're always losing and miserable, then you are not practicing the Daishonin's Buddhism correctly. You are not following the true path in life. Buddhism teaches the means by which the sad become happy and the happy become happier still. That is the reason for our practice. (5/19/97)

Buddhism teaches the principle that earthly desires are enlightenment. To explain this very simply, earthly desires refers to suffering and to the desires and cravings that cause suffering, while enlightenment refers to attaining a vast, expansive state of absolute happiness. Normally, one would assume that earthly desires and enlightenment are separate and distinct especially since suffering would seem to be the exact opposite of happiness. But Nichiren Daishonin's Buddhism teaches that only by igniting the firewood of earthly desires can the flame of happiness be attained. Through chanting daimoku, we burn this firewood of earthly desires. (DOY 2, ch. 19)

The wonderful thing about Nichiren Daishonin's Buddhism is that, through daimoku, the four sufferings of birth, aging, sickness and death can be transformed into four castle walls or ramparts that fortify the palace of your life. The mud of our suffering provides the building material from which we can erect a solid bulwark for our palace of happiness within. (DOY 2, ch. 20)

President Toda used the term *absolute happiness* to describe the state of mind in which we feel that life itself is a joy. If you persevere in faith, you will definitely come to experience this state of mind. (DOY 2, ch. 20)

HEALTH

Life possesses the mysterious power not only to transform the negative into a neutral state but to go beyond that to achieve a positive state. We overcome the suffering of sickness and in so doing even the experience of sickness enriches our lives and makes them more worthwhile, providing the material for a great drama of fulfillment that unfolds day after day. (2/23/90)

～

Sickness is not merely a physical phenomenon; it invariably signals the presence of spiritual malady, too. In seeking to cure someone's illness, we should spare no effort, leave no stone unturned. (LG, p. 145)

～

We are all mortal flesh and blood. Everyone at some time suffers from illness in one form or another. The power of the Mystic Law enables us to bring forth strength to overcome the pain and suffering of sickness with courage and determination. (6/15/96)

～

Nichiren Daishonin says, "A hundred years of practice in the land of Perfect Bliss cannot compare to the benefit gained from one day's practice in this impure world" (MW-4, 272). An awareness of how precious each life and each day is produces hope that increases our life force, our benefits and our healing power. (7/27/91)

～

When you cling to one set idea, you can't respond to changes. Most people think that illnesses should be left entirely up to doctors. There is a certain degree of truth in that assumption, but I also believe that we can respond to illness by realizing that we ourselves are not only the patient but, to some extent, our own doctors as well. (2/21/90)

It has been found that a person becomes vulnerable to cancer following the spiritual shock accompanying the death of someone important, such as a husband, wife or child. The inability to express sadness, anxiety or anger, suppressing emotions, losing hope and experiencing melancholia all tend to support the development of cancer or slow recovery in those already battling the disease. If, on the other hand, you have discovered new meaning in life and have a strong will to live, striving toward new goals, cancer cells will be exterminated. (7/27/91)

It has been reported that practicing a religion plays a vital role in shrinking cancer cells. According to a report, about one-third of the cancer patients studied had experienced the agony of loneliness in their infancy from losing parents or loved ones. The report says that such negative experiences form spiritual stress and can trigger cancer. Loss of someone you love is the most powerful kind of stress. Those who encountered someone who gave them parental love, however, were able to release this spiritual stress, reducing the number of cancer cells. Some contend that encountering an excellent religion also makes this possible. (7/27/91)

There have been many reports from all over the world of spontaneous remission or disappearance of cancer. One doctor in New York researched the phenomenon and declared that spontaneous cures were not mere coincidence. He clearly asserted that a substantial change of outlook, a dramatic inner change within the patient, checked the progress of cancer cells. The progress of the disease always depended on whether the patient had a strong desire to win in the face of the crisis. (7/27/91)

~

Needless to say, early discovery and early treatment are pre-requisites in the battle against cancer. Much progress has been made in methods of treatment, such as operations, chemotherapy, radiation therapy and immunization. A patient's hope-filled, strong will is the key to maximizing the effects of these therapies. (7/27/91)

~

If you develop cancer, do not become angry or hateful. Do not feel sad or sorry for yourself. Instead, always burn with hope and a sense of mission based on faith and maintain strong willpower; such a person can win over illness and make the struggle against sickness more effective and even encouraging. (7/27/91)

~

Taking good care of our health is most important. In particular, it is vital for those who are advanced in years to get sufficient rest to avoid becoming fatigued. Sleep is the best medicine. I also hope you will put your wisdom to work and find various ways to improve and maintain your health. (5/17/95)

~

It is only natural that sometimes we fall sick. But we must see that as a sickness that exists originally in life, based on the principle of the Mystic Law. In other words, there is no reason to allow yourself to be controlled by illness, for it to fill your life with suffering and distress. From the standpoint of eternal life through the three existences, your fundamentally happy self is incontrovertibly established. (2/20/90)

The great American poet Walt Whitman writes in *Leaves of Grass*: "All comes by the body, only health puts you rapport with the universe." I am sure you are all very busy, but I hope you will advance in good health and with optimism and enjoy the power of your faith, which is what puts you in rhythm with the universe. (2/7/96)

Everyone at some time suffers from illness in one form or another. The power of the Mystic Law enables us to bring forth strength to overcome the pain and suffering of sickness with courage and new determination. (6/15/96)

The moment we resolve "I will become healthy!" "I will become strong!" "I will work cheerfully for kosen-rufu!" our lives begin to move in that direction. We have to make up our minds first. (7/12/95)

INTELLECT

Just as Nikko Shonin states, without an understanding of both Buddhist and non-Buddhist writings, neither realizing peace ("securing the land") nor accomplishing kosen-rufu ("establishing the Buddhist Law") will be possible. In addition, Nikko Shonin indicates that capable people who are well versed in both realms [of Buddhist and secular knowledge] are necessary. In particular, young people, basing themselves on Buddhism, must study hard, avidly seeking to expand their grasp of the knowledge and wisdom of the world. (10/1/91)

If your physical health is poor, both you and your family will suffer. Without sound mental capabilities, you cannot see the truth and thereby will be too easily deceived by evil. Nor can you create any great value in society. It is imperative that you have wisdom. For that reason it is vital that, based on chanting daimoku, you study diligently, starting with the Daishonin's teachings. It is essential that you develop and strengthen your intellect. (2/19/93)

Faith is the ultimate essence of intellect. Through the practice of correct faith, the intellect will shine. Intellect without correct faith lacks a firm anchor in the soil of life and eventually becomes disordered. This prompted the first Soka Gakkai president, Tsunesaburo Makiguchi, to remark that many modern thinkers were suffering from what he termed "higher psychosis." Faith without intellect, meanwhile, leads to blind faith and fanaticism. Faith or intellect alone—one without the other—is unhealthy. (1/28/93)

To establish meaningful lives, I hope that during your youth you will work hard to polish your intellect. Life, in a sense, is a battle of wisdom. It is the power of Buddhism that enables one to win this battle. True faith is characterized by a brilliance of intellect and depth of wisdom that result from devotion to practice. (2/22/90)

Buddhism teaches that "all phenomena in the universe are manifestations of the Law" (*Gosho Zenshu,* p. 564). I hope you will, with this understanding, engage yourselves in broad-ranging studies with vigor and determination. Your brains have a potential as vast and boundless as the universe. How then do we manifest the brain's full creative powers? There is only one way to bring out our full intellectual capacity: by constantly putting our minds to work. (4/2/98)

Intellect will play a very important role in the coming age. By intellect I mean refined wisdom, clear reasoning, profound philosophy and broad-ranging knowledge. We are entering an age when people will develop intelligence and wisdom, infusing society with their new outlooks. (2/13/90)

JOB/CAREER

Mr. Makiguchi taught that there are three kinds of value: beauty, benefit and good. In the working world the value of beauty means to find a job you like; the value of benefit is to get a job that earns you a salary that can support your daily life; the value of good means to find a job that helps others and contributes to society. (DOY 1, ch. 8)

President Toda said that the most important thing is to first become indispensable wherever you are. Instead of moaning that a job differs from what you'd like to be doing, he said, become a first-class individual at that job. This will open the path leading to your next phase in life, during which you should also continue doing your best. Such continuous efforts are guaranteed to land you a job that you like, that supports your life, and that allows you to contribute to society. (DOY 1, ch. 8)

Once you have decided on a job, I hope you will not be the kind of people who quit at the drop of a hat and are always insecure and complaining. Nevertheless, if after you've given it your all you decide that your job isn't right for you and you move on, that's perfectly all right, too. My concern is that you don't forget that you are responsible for your environment when you make your decision. (DOY 1, ch. 8)

There is a saying that urges us, "Excel at something!" It is important to become trusted by others wherever you are and to shine with excellence. Sometimes people may dislike their job at first but grow to love it once they become serious about doing their best. "What one likes, one will do well," goes another saying. Growing to like your job will also enable you to develop your talent. (DOY 1, ch. 8)

When working in a company—which is like a society or community all its own—it is important to create harmonious relations with your colleagues and superiors, using wisdom and discretion along the way. If you incur your co-workers' dislike by being selfish or egotistic, you will be a loser in work and society. Wisdom is vital to being successful at one's work. The Daishonin writes, "The wise may be called human, but the thoughtless are no more than animals" (MW-2 [2nd ed.], 240). (DOY 1, ch. 8)

Love and Relationships

I hope that those of you who are wives will cherish your husbands, that those of you who are husbands will cherish your wives, and that, throughout your lives, you will strive to create at home and in your friendships an atmosphere imbued with a sense of mutual respect and mutual encouragement. (9/29/91)

If you are neglecting things you should be doing, forgetting your purpose in life because of the relationship you're in, then you're on the wrong path. A healthy relationship is one in which two people encourage each other to reach their respective goals while sharing each other's hopes and dreams. A relationship should be a source of inspiration, invigoration and hope. (DOY 1, ch. 7)

Love should be a force that helps you expand your lives and bring forth your innate potential with fresh and dynamic vitality. That is the ideal, but as the saying "love is blind" illustrates, people often lose all objectivity when they fall in love. (DOY 1, ch. 7)

Men should always remember to be extremely courteous and caring toward women. They should respect women, doing their utmost to support them. Men should become strong enough, compassionate enough and adult enough to care about the lifelong happiness of their partners. This is the quality men must strive to cultivate; it is also an expression of true love. (DOY 1, ch. 7)

Rather than becoming so love-struck that you create a world where only the two of you exist, it is much healthier to learn from those qualities of your partner that you respect and admire and make efforts to improve and develop yourself. Antoine de Saint-Exupéry, the author of *The Little Prince*, once wrote, "Love is not two people gazing at each other, but two

people looking ahead together in the same direction." It follows then that relationships last longer when both partners
share similar values and beliefs. (DOY 1, ch. 7)

Real love is not two people clinging to each other; it can
only be fostered between two strong people secure in their
individuality. A shallow person will have only shallow relationships. If you want to experience real love, it is important
to first sincerely develop a strong self-identity. (DOY 1, ch. 7)

What is friendship? True friendship implies a relationship
where you empathize with your friends when they're suffering and encourage them not to lose heart, and where they, in
turn, empathize with you when you're in the same situation
and try to cheer you up. A friendship with those qualities
flows as beautifully as a pure, fresh stream. (DOY 1, ch. 6)

Buddhism lists the suffering of parting from one's loved ones
as one of the eight types of suffering. In life, we will encounter separations of inexpressible sadness. However, those
who overcome such grief and continue to live with strength
and courage will be cherished and respected by their juniors
as kings and queens of life. There is no more lofty life than
that of one who surmounts personal tragedy and leaves behind some achievement for future generations. (10/1/91)

The important thing is to overcome the sorrow that accom-
panies any type of separation, such as death or divorce. The
vital thing is to continue advancing. Do not look back. Just
forge on. There are many reasons why people bid farewell to
one another. People have their own thoughts and situations.

It may be difficult indeed not to look back. The deep scars within your heart may not heal quickly. Yet brace yourself so you can look forward. You have to advance, even a step. You should strive to move on, cutting through the clouds in your heart. As long as you advance, new hope will be born. The sun will rise. Only when you continue to advance can you encounter an even better, more wonderful you. A new life will unfold for you. (Editorial, 3/21/97 WT)

Those who realize their own shortcomings and then chant daimoku while striving to improve themselves will definitely see their lives change. Someone who is quiet and introverted, for instance, may come to shine as being thoughtful and discrete. Usually, in the long run, such people tend to develop closer, deeper friendships than their louder, extroverted peers, who sometimes tend to act before they think! (DOY 1, ch. 6)

It is quite rare for the individual and the state to come into direct confrontation; the vast majority of our time is spent in "smaller-scale" situations—at home, in the workplace or local community. These settings are the sites for our face-to-face, genuine engagement with others and as such are the sites of self-discoveries, because here we acutely sense the reality of our existence and come to appreciate the joys of life and living. (1/30/91)

Divorce is, of course, a private matter about which only the parties involved can decide. From the Buddhist perspective, it is impossible to build personal happiness on the sufferings of others, and they should bear this in mind as they make their decision. It is through sometimes painful reflection and forbearance required to face head-on a difficult situation that the internal workings of the conscience can be strengthened and disciplined, enabling those concerned to minimize the sundering and destruction of human relationships that might otherwise result. (9/26/91)

MEN

"Why aren't the men more enthusiastic?" women's division members ask. I say that the men's division members *are* enthusiastic; they just don't make a show of it. They want to surprise everyone with a brilliant achievement—like the quiet man who turns out to be a hero at the climax of a great drama.

Others ask, "Why are they so reluctant to act?" I say that the men *aren't* reluctant; they are prudent. They don't want to waste their efforts. They know the importance of waiting until the time is ripe.

"Why are they so timid?" asks another. "Why don't they speak up?" I say that they're *not* timid; they're just thoughtful. They choose their words carefully, out of consideration for others and to avoid meaningless babble. (Essay, 7/10/98 WT)

It was in his 40s that Shijo Kingo traveled all the way to visit and seek guidance from the Daishonin in his exile on Sado Island. He went on to prove the justice and power of Buddhism despite the adverse circumstances of having his fief confiscated. In this sense, we may say that Shijo Kingo was a pioneering member of the men's division, rather than the youth division. (Essay, 7/10/98 WT)

The men's division members are lions. Their indomitable presence gives assurance to those around them. When their resolute voices ring out, they instill courage in everyone and bring about victory for the people. (Essay, 7/10/98 WT)

The men's division members are the cornerstones of the Soka Gakkai. They are runners in the relay race of kosen-rufu, the last runners who determine our victory or defeat. (Essay, 7/10/98 WT)

My heroic [men's division] friends! My noble comrades in the struggle for kosen-rufu! A decisive battle to usher in the dawn of the twenty-first century has already begun. At last, our time has come. If we do not rise to the challenge now, then when? If we do not fight today, then when? (Essay, 7/10/98 WT)

Men and women are equal. People who ignore this in their behavior cannot be called civilized. It sometimes happens that if women blindly follow male leaders, all will wind up suffering in the end. Rather, Buddhism teaches that women and men should complement one another like a bow and arrow. In order that the arrow may proceed along the correct path, a correct direction for the bow must be set and from time to time adjustments made. (2/21/90)

Our efforts, even if no one else is aware of them, are communicated to the Gohonzon. But there are some—notably men, I gather from the women's division—who though they understand this in theory have difficulty getting it right in practice. Therefore, I would be most delighted if women, rather than being reactive, would try to subtly redirect these men toward faith by setting a sterling example themselves. (2/24/96)

Men can be pretentious or, in a word, vain. Men, they say, tend to feign knowledge when they don't have a clue; they let on to have ability when they do not; they pretend to have money when they are broke; and they try to pass themselves off as great when nothing could be further from the truth. Unfortunately, such pretentiousness is entirely transparent to the sharp eyes of women! (2/24/96)

Men and women are completely equal. However, we can still identify tendencies exhibited by members of each sex. I would like our men to be brave and upright individuals, capable people who can protect others. I would like our women to be blessed above all with happiness and good fortune. To achieve that, they must have pure hearts. (2/3/93)

We of the SGI must learn from women, defend their rights and, more than anywhere else in the world, accord women the highest respect and consideration. Men who scold women out of emotionalism are contemptible. (1/31/93)

PARENTS

Please do not forget your mother's love or the hardships she has endured for you. I am confident that while people keep the memory of their mothers' loving face alive in their minds, they will never go astray. Similarly, as long as we bear in mind the Daishonin's profound compassion and live in deep appreciation of it, our lives will be illuminated by the light of Buddhahood. (2/22/90)

You may wonder why you were born into your family, or why your parents aren't as kind as others, or why you are not blessed with a more beautiful home and a better family. You may even want to run away from home. But the fact is you were born to this particular family, in this particular place and on this planet Earth. You were not born into any other family. This fact encompasses the meaning of everything. (DOY 1, ch. 2)

Many of your parents have devoted their lives to the SGI's struggle for humanity. Desiring neither fame nor status, they strive with selfless love for humanity, for the benefit of all. They live in the muddy pond of this perverse society but hold a beautiful, pristine ideal above it. They are noble men and women. (DOY 2, ch. 1)

I would ask the members of the youth division, in particular, to practice with the spirit to demonstrate to their parents that they are growing and becoming fine human beings. Please have the broad perspective that it's okay to save sharing Buddhism with your parents for last. The wisest course is to place the greatest importance on your own growth and human development. (2/24/96)

The Lotus Sutra is a teaching of the highest filial piety. The Daishonin deeply praised the faith of Sennichi-ama in offering prayers in memory of her deceased father, and he sent her the precious gift of a copy of the Lotus Sutra in ten volumes

(Ref. MW-6, 257). Through our practice of the Mystic Law, we can bring the greatest imaginable benefit to our parents, whether or not they practice, whether they are still alive or have passed away. Please be confident on this point. (6/15/96)

The Lotus Sutra expounds the oneness and simultaneous enlightenment of parent and child. Children, through faith, can definitely cause their parents to attain Buddhahood. In this scenario, from the parent's perspective the child is not merely a child but what Buddhism calls a "good friend," someone who leads another to Buddhism. In the same way, the child can also attain Buddhahood through the parent's faith. It all depends on the parent's resolute faith and nothing else. It is important that we have unshakable confidence in this. (LG, p. 167)

We should chant with the determination to lead our children, as well as our parents, to happiness and complete fulfillment. Each daimoku we chant with such determination becomes a brilliant sun illuminating the lives of our children or parents, transcending great distances and even the threshold of life and death. (LG, p. 167)

No one is more wonderful than a mother. And there is nothing more noble than a mother's heart. I hope you will all treasure your mothers. Truly praiseworthy are those who have a sense of gratitude and appreciation toward their parents. The Buddhist sutras teach that the practice of Buddhism is the ultimate expression of devotion to one's parents, and the Buddha excels in such dedication and concern. (5/3/96)

When parents exert themselves in the way of faith, they can lead their children to happiness without fail. Likewise, the child's attainment of Buddhahood guarantees the parents' attainment of Buddhahood. One lighthouse illuminates the way for many ships to steer a course safely through uncertain waters. In the same way, people with strong and committed faith shine as beacons of hope for their family and relatives. (4/23/96)

RAISING CHILDREN

A mother's beliefs have a powerful influence on her children. In the realm of Nichiren Daishonin's Buddhism, the children of families where the mother's faith is strong invariably develop into admirable adults. (7/19/96)

Someone who embraces faith is never isolated. The heart can communicate without fail. The same is true of education in the home. It may be that you cannot always be with your children. However, the most noble thing for parents is to proudly teach their children a way of life of altruism and dedication to Buddhism, conveying this spirit through their lives. Forming strong heart-to-heart bonds with your children is the key to education in the home that produces outstanding individuals. (LG, p. 118)

People wanting to have a child may tend to imagine that if only they could they would be happy. But—as the Daishonin indicates when he says that a child may become a parent's enemy—countless people become miserable on account of their children. Happiness or unhappiness in life does not hinge on whether we have children. (LG, p. 168)

Those who do not have children can love and look after that many more children of the Buddha with the same parental affection they would show their own children. This is most worthy of respect. (LG, p. 168)

Some agonize because they cannot have children. And they may be deeply hurt by someone even casually needling them about "starting a family." When it comes to such highly personal matters, we should exercise great sensitivity and discretion. (LG, p. 168)

The good fortune that accrues to parents who apply themselves diligently to SGI activities will protect their children without fail. Based on this conviction, you must still make positive efforts to open and sustain dialogue with your children, not allowing yourselves to neglect them, claiming that you're too busy or it can't be helped, or telling yourselves that somehow things will be taken care of. Unless you make such positive efforts, you are irresponsible parents who lack compassion. (2/3/93)

Sometimes your children may not be able to do gongyo, but there is no reason for parents to become overly concerned or agitated about this. There are times when chanting only three daimoku is sufficient. To continue practicing [even though gongyo may not be consistent] is far more important. What matters is that the children maintain their connection to the Gohonzon and the SGI for their entire lives. (2/3/93)

Putting too much pressure on children to practice may only alienate them from faith. Lead them wisely so that they will mature in the best direction, in a relaxed and natural manner. (2/3/93)

I would like to request that, no matter how busy you may be, you find the time to get together to talk with your children. The length of time is not important. What matters is that parents use their wisdom. (2/3/93)

When you have to be away from home for some reason, try to leave a note for your children or call them on the phone when you have a chance. The important thing is to make sure that you stay in communication with them in some form. Children come home. They don't know where their parents are. No message is waiting for them. Naturally, they're bound to feel lonely, to feel emotionally insecure. This is a heartless way to treat children. You must not subject them to such loneliness. (2/3/93)

Even if it's only a brief meeting, give your children a hug when you see them. Touch them and talk to them. Try to make time to listen to what they have to say. As long as you have love and compassion, you will find the wisdom to make this work. The desire to save others becomes merely an abstract goal if those who practice faith cannot communicate with their own children nor build strong and happy families. (2/3/93)

A child is a person, an individual with his or her distinct personality. Sometimes children can be even more keenly perceptive than adults. That is why we must be careful how we behave in front of them. If parents must fight, go off where they can't see you! (2/3/93)

~

Children are saddened when their parents fight. They go off to school with heavy hearts, and they won't forget the incident for a long time. Tall trees grow from secure and solid ground. Please give your children a home where they can enjoy tranquility and peace of mind. (2/3/93)

~

Sons tend to rebel when scolded by their fathers, while they are more likely to listen to their mother's scolding. The worst thing is for the father and the mother to gang up and together scold the child. This leaves the child with no one to whom he or she can turn. (2/3/93)

~

Fathers tend to have a soft spot for daughters and, consequently, are too easy on them. Mothers and daughters, meanwhile, often share a deep, natural understanding as women. That is why it is often better for mothers to discipline their daughters. (2/3/93)

~

Mr. Toda said: When fathers grow angry, they alienate their children. But even when a mother gets angry, her children stay close to her. This wisdom is based on the laws of human behavior, the laws of life and psychology. (2/3/93)

~

Children who may be suffering a disadvantage compared to their peers need our encouragement all the more. Watch over these children with affection and encourage them. Discover their strengths and praise them for those, building their confidence. Become their unfailing ally, support them, shower them with love and believe utterly in their potential. That is a parent's role. (2/3/93)

The Daishonin likens the selfless love of a mother for her off-spring to the compassionate actions of a bodhisattva and the majestic power of the heavenly god Bonten. He says that if the mother takes faith in the Mystic Law, her love for her children will surely be communicated to the Gohonzon and enable both the mother and child to reach the world of Buddhahood. (2/21/90)

Ours is the noblest way of life. We must make sure our children understand and respect our beliefs, our way of life and our dedication. It is a mistake to assume that they will somehow come to know we love them or to understand our commitment to kosen-rufu without us having to say anything. (2/3/93)

We must make conscious efforts to verbalize and communicate our thoughts and feelings to our children and to do so wisely, in a relaxed and open manner, without undue haste. Finding the wisdom for this task is an expression of our faith. (2/3/93)

READING

Learning is a lifelong process. Crucial is the determination to make the wisdom passed down through the ages your own.

I'm going to read thousands of books! That's the kind of enthusiasm that you should have. (DOY 2, ch. 13)

Reading makes us human. No matter how high people's positions are, if they haven't read great novels by the world's renowned authors, they can never hope to become outstanding leaders. (DOY 2, ch. 13)

Those who know the great joy of reading have richer lives and broader perspectives than those who don't. You can travel east, west, north and south and become acquainted with new people and places in books. Reading transcends time. You can go on an expedition with Alexander the Great or become friends with people like Socrates or Victor Hugo and hold dialogues with them. (DOY 2, ch. 13)

We must read in a way that nourishes and cultivates us. Food will not nourish us or contribute to healthy bone and muscle growth if it is not digested and absorbed properly. Similarly, digesting what we read requires serious reflection and contemplation. (DOY 2, ch. 13)

Someone once described bad books as messengers of degeneracy, guides to delinquency, traps to misery and insidious poison. Good books, on the other hand, are as wonderful as an amazing teacher, a trusted confidant or a parent. They contain a wellspring of wisdom, a fountain of life, bright illumination and human goodness. (DOY 2, ch. 13)

There is no limit to your potential if the earth of your minds is cultivated and well-nourished. Within each of you lies a vast field of infinite possibility. And reading is the hoe with which to till the soil of that boundless frontier. (DOY 2, ch. 13)

Only human beings have the ability to read. I'm sure that some people think that they'll start reading later in life when they have more time. But chances are that if you neglect reading during your youth, you won't read later on either. For that reason, it's important to get into the habit of reading while you are young. This will establish a foundation on which to build the rest of your life. I cannot stress this enough. (DOY 2, ch. 13)

Encountering a great book is like encountering a great teacher. Reading is a privilege only human beings have. Through reading, we come into contact with hundreds and thousands of lives and commune with sages and philosophers from as long as two millennia ago. (DOY 2, ch. 13)

Almost without exception great people had a book they held dear during their youth—a book that served as their guide and as a source of encouragement; as a close friend and mentor. (DOY 2, ch. 13)

Books introduce you to the fragrant flowers of life, to rivers, roads and adventures. You can find stars and light, feel delight and indignation. You are set adrift on a vast sea of emotion in a ship of reason, moved by the infinite breeze of poetry.

Dreams and dramas evolve. The whole world comes alive. (DOY 2, ch. 13)

To gain true satisfaction and pleasure from anything requires some kind of practice, training and effort. You cannot fully enjoy skiing without working at it. It also takes effort, perseverance and patience to appreciate reading. Those who have tasted this joy, who have looked on books as friends, are strong. . . . (DOY 2, ch. 13)

Reading gives you free access to the treasures of the human spirit from all ages and from all parts of the world. One who knows this possesses unsurpassed wealth. It's like owning countless banks from which you can make unlimited withdrawals. . . . (DOY 2, ch. 13)

When you're head over heels for someone, you want to see him or her whenever and wherever you can, even if it's only a brief glance or just for five minutes, right? That should be our attitude toward reading. . . . (DOY 2, ch. 13)

Reading is like mountain climbing. Ascending a steep summit is quite difficult, but how great is your exhilaration when you've successfully conquered it. . . . (DOY 2, ch. 13)

SCHOOL

Young people in school should make study their first priority. It goes without saying that faith is important, but faith is something we practice throughout our entire lives. There is a certain period and age when we should study. If we don't work hard during that period, we may fail to acquire important knowledge and skills, and we may come to regret it deeply later. Faith manifests itself in daily life. For young people in school, faith manifests itself in their studies. During this period, to devote themselves to study represents an important part of their practice of faith. (2/3/93)

If study ends up robbing people of their humanity, its purpose is completely destroyed. Studying is important, of course, but the real purpose of study is to enrich oneself as a human being, to make valuable contributions that will benefit many people. (DOY 2, ch. 12)

I hope you will all become people who can wholeheartedly, honestly say of your youth that you read as much as you could and gave your all to your studies! (DOY 2, ch. 13)

SELF-IDENTITY

Human beings are always influenced by their immediate environment. If you surround yourself with good influences you will improve; if you associate with bad influences you will change for the worse. It is therefore important to establish a self-identity that will take you toward positive influences and leave you impervious to negative influences, so that you can continue striving in a positive direction, no matter what happens. The key lies in whether you can create good, value and happiness in any situation. (8/7/92)

Where on earth is happiness to be found? How can we become happy? These are fundamental questions in life, and human beings will no doubt be destined to pursue them eternally. The teachings of Buddhism and faith in the Mystic Law provide fundamental answers to these questions. Ultimately, happiness rests on how you establish your own solid self or sense of being. (6/23/96)

∽

It is important that you concentrate on developing yourself. Whatever others may say or do, those who have established their own solid sense of identity will triumph in the end. The great Japanese author Eiji Yoshikawa (1892–1962) wrote in his novel *Miyamoto Musashi* [an account of the seventeenth-century master swordsman of the same name]: "Rather than worrying about your future, thinking 'Perhaps I should become this or perhaps I should become that,' first be still and build a self that is as solid and unmoving as Mount Fuji." (4/17/96)

∽

The Mystic Law embodying the principle of "revealing one's intrinsic nature" enables all human beings to shine with their greatest possible brilliance, to reveal their true and highest potential. This is one of the underlying principles of our SGI movement. (1/30/93)

SELF-RELIANCE

What was Napoleon's motto? One of his mottoes appears to have been taken from the ancient Greek philosopher Epictetus (*ca* A.D. 55–135): "If someone speaks ill of you and what he says is true, then correct yourself. If it's a lie, then laugh about it." This reasoning is simple and clear. Hence, Napoleon declared:

"I have learned not to be surprised. I know my place, and I don't trouble over the dogs that bark along my path." (2/24/96)

Great victors in life are those who have developed a strong sense of self that allows them to say, "I may receive no praise, but I am satisfied." (DOY 1, ch. 2)

Gandhi taught people to live with lionlike courage, impressing upon them that they could not afford to leave things up to others, that they had to stand up for themselves and fight for justice. Ultimately, the only way forward is by developing self-reliance, forging a stand-alone spirit. That is the only path to victory. (2/3/98)

Our lives are our own. It is not for someone else to dictate to us how we should live. All that awaits those who allow themselves to be continually swayed by what other people say or do is unhappiness. We simply need to have the self-belief to be able to say: "This is right. This is the path I will follow. I am content." Happiness is born from such inner fortitude. Moreover, those who earnestly devote themselves in accord with the Mystic Law cannot fail to realize lives of total fulfillment. (3/18/96)

Many religions have demanded blind faith, taking away people's independence. President Makiguchi opposed such enslavement. What he called for instead was the solidarity of awakened common people. To achieve this he proposed a self-reliant way of life in which we advance on the path of our choice with a firm, independent character. He also stressed a contributive way of life in which we set our fundamental goal in life toward the realization of happiness for ourselves and others, casting aside arrogance and self-satisfaction to respect and benefit others. (1/29/95)

"Don't be dependent on anyone"—this is my sentiment. We each have to strengthen and develop ourselves through our own efforts. We must never surrender to any foe or difficulty. We must be fearless. This is the true spirit of self-reliance. (5/19/97)

SUCCESS

You are worthy of the highest respect. You are noble leaders who are praised and protected by Nichiren Daishonin and the Buddhas and bodhisattvas of the ten directions. Right now you may be unknown. You may have no money. You may be laughed at and ridiculed by people ignorant of the Daishonin's Buddhism. But when viewed from the perspective of the eternity of life you are all supreme victors, people who will achieve unsurpassed success in life. There is no doubt that in future existences each of you will enjoy an expansive life-condition far surpassing that of presidents, business tycoons or eminent scholars. Nichiren Daishonin assures us of this in his writings. If it were not true the Daishonin would be a liar. And that just isn't possible. The Daishonin never lies. (7/11/99)

One kind of actual proof of victory in daily life is financial security. I hope, therefore, as you accumulate bountiful treasures of the heart and much good fortune, that you will also become secure financially. As long as we are living and working in society, having a certain amount of financial security is an important element for happiness. (9/26/93)

The second Soka Gakkai president, Josei Toda, used to say, even though your wallet may be empty, there is an abundance of money floating about in the world—it just hasn't come your way, that's all! But, he would continue, if you accumulate good fortune, using it to "drill a hole" into that vast reservoir of money and tap some for yourself, you will never have to be wanting. (9/26/93)

A tree doesn't grow strong and tall within one or two days. In the same way, successful people didn't get to where they are in only one or two years. This applies to everything. (DOY 1, ch. 8)

In too many cases, acquiring fame, status or wealth alters a person's character. It is as though the person turns into a puppet of fame or wealth. How can human beings live in accordance with their unchanging innermost self and not be affected by these influences? Herein lies the battle of human life; such is the path believers in the Mystic Law must follow. (1/6/91)

Success is not a matter of accumulating more of this or that; it is not measured in quantity. It means changing the *quality* of your life. Wealth, power, fame and knowledge alone cannot make you happy, no matter how much of these you acquire. Nor can you take them with you when you die. But by

improving the quality of your life you will at last approach
true happiness. (3/5/97)

The only way to succeed is by first bringing to completion
that which is most immediate. This principle applies in all affairs—in our daily lives, our work and our families, as well as
in the progress of kosen-rufu. (2/17/90)

Buddhist scriptures describe secular millionaires as being of a
good family, possessing wealth, having dignity, being pure in
their actions, exhibiting proper manners and enjoying great
prestige. In accordance with the teaching that "all laws are the
Buddhist Law," it is worthwhile for us to strive to acquire the
virtues of these millionaires. I hope that, basing yourselves on
faith, you will become wealthy people of virtue and influence
who are widely respected. (2/18/90)

What is success in life? Who are the truly successful? There
are famous and powerful people who become pitiful figures
in their old age. There are people who die alone, feeling empty and desolate inside. Just what is success? The English
thinker Walter Pater (1839–94) wrote: "To burn always with
this hard, gemlike flame, to maintain this ecstasy, is success in
life." The person who lives life fully, glowing with life's energy, is the person who lives a successful life. (3/5/97)

Such things as money, fame and material possessions offer
fleeting satisfactions that can be called relative happiness.
However, when we transform our lives internally, when we
develop within ourselves a brilliant inner palace, then we can

be said to have established absolute happiness. (DOY 2, ch. 20)

A person of success in the true sense is one who can enjoy a free and unrestrained state of life. (2/18/90)

You who have embraced this great Law are millionaires rich in life force who possess good fortune surpassing the wealth of even the world's richest people. Material possessions cannot be enjoyed after death. But "millionaires rich in life force" can freely make use of the treasures of the universe in lifetime after lifetime and enjoy a journey of eternal happiness. (2/18/90)

Worldly success is not equivalent to true happiness. Achieving this requires that we have a profound understanding of the nature of life. There is much truth to the words of Benjamin Franklin that "success has ruined many a man." (2/18/90)

There is nothing wrong with being successful in society and enjoying a degree of fame. But ultimately, the lives of those dedicated to the welfare and happiness of others, even if they remain unrecognized, are the ones truly worthy of respect. (DOY 1, ch. 2)

SUCCESSORS

This is the era of youth. Youth do not depend on anyone. Nor do they hang on someone else's coattails. "I will open the way forward myself. I will advance kosen-rufu. I will see to it that the SGI is victorious." This is the spirit of youth and the attitude of true successors who love and cherish the SGI. (9/25/97)

There is a saying, "To start an undertaking is easy; to maintain it is difficult." Though creating something new may seem daunting, it is in fact easy when compared to the far more challenging task of carrying on an existing enterprise, to keep it going, to develop it further. Everything depends on people, on capable successors. And our movement for kosen-rufu depends on young people. For that reason I am determined to do all that I can right now to raise genuine successors in the youth division. (1/17/98)

TREASURES OF THE HEART

The treasure of the heart is the most fundamental treasure. In this sense, all of you who spare no effort in exerting yourselves day and night for the sake of the Law and for the sake of others are people of character who possess the greatest happiness in life. The treasure of the heart that is faith is an eternal treasure that adorns our lives over the three existences of past, present and future. (6/11/92)

Writes Goethe: "My intelligence and talent are held with higher esteem than my heart. But my heart is my sole pride.... The things I know anyone can know. But I am the only one who can possess my heart." Similarly, the Daishonin teaches that the heart is what matters most and urges us to accumulate the treasures of the heart, which are the most valuable of all. With this spirit, let us strive to create lives of unsurpassed richness. (3/8/96)

As you make your way home tonight, may you pause for a moment to gaze up at the night sky and let your heart communicate with the moon in wordless dialogue. Perhaps you might compose a poem to set down in your journal entry for today. I would like you to possess such a poetic spirit. (3/24/97)

TRUE FREEDOM

The inner liberation and blossoming of human life—these are the goals that a Buddhist aims to realize. A Buddhist is the spring breeze of humanity that melts away the ice of authority chilling people's hearts. Truly, Buddhists are "emissaries of spring" who actualize a renaissance in themselves and others. (1/16/91)

When people become spiritually bankrupt, society turns into a kind of hell where there is no freedom and where people can no longer live as human beings. For precisely this reason, it is imperative that the inner prison in people's lives be destroyed. One must not give in to it or accept it as inevitable. (3/27/91)

Kings and queens, for instance, possess tremendous treasures that enable them to lead lives of total ease and comfort, wanting for nothing. Likewise, as kings and queens of faith, you possess boundless treasures in your heart. You need only bring forth the treasure appropriate to the situation and complete fulfillment will be yours. You will experience a state of life of total freedom. Such is the wondrous and inscrutable function of the Mystic Law. (1/30/93)

John Dewey, whom President Makiguchi held in high esteem, finds freedom within growth and development. He states: "We are free not because of what we statically are, but inasfar as we are becoming different from what we have been." People of genuine freedom are those who continue to grow and develop, who continue to keep themselves fresh and new. In that respect, I heartily rejoice at the hope-filled future that lies in store for all of you. (6/15/96)

VICTORY

Buddhism stresses the importance of being victorious. Life, too, is a struggle for victory. Chanting daimoku is the fundamental determinant of victory. Nothing can match the power of daimoku. As long as we persevere in chanting daimoku, we have nothing to fear. (1/6/96)

President Toda often said that the final four or five years of one's life are decisive. No matter how good the preceding years may have been, one's life ends in defeat and sadness if the final few years are miserable. On the other hand, someone whose last four or five years are happy and filled with joy can be described as a winner in life. No matter what happens, even if we should fall sick, we must never grow discouraged or allow ourselves to be defeated. This is vital. As long as our spirits are undefeated, we are victors. (9/15/97)

We must gain decisive victory over the harsh realities of society and lead a correct and vibrant life. This is the purpose
of our faith. We have to become wise and strong. (2/27/90)

March 16, Kosen-rufu Day. The spirit of this day lives not in
magnificent ceremonies or high-sounding words. It lives in
victory. Victory is the most crucial thing in all endeavors. In
life and in kosen-rufu, we either win or lose. I would like you
to be absolute victors in both. No matter what excuses we try
to make, giving in to defeat brings misery and loses us the respect of others. I hope each of you without exception will
adorn your life with indestructible triumph. (3/13/98)

We live in turbulent times. There seems to be no reliable standard these days for distinguishing between right and wrong.
Pure-hearted young people with high ideals cannot help but
be disturbed and troubled by such inadequacies. While it is
naturally important that you make efforts to change society,
you must also be victors in daily life. Buddhism is a struggle
to be victorious. So is life. Only by winning in life can we become happy. (1/26/96)

Victory is not easily won. If it is, it will not be a source of
pride. What possible gratification, for instance, could a sumo
wrestler derive from defeating a child? Only when we fight
and win over dire circumstances will our victory shine brilliantly in history. (2/14/90)

President Toda used to say, "Become individuals who are
strong physically, intellectually and spiritually." To be strong in
all three areas is the ideal. Many people may be strong in one

or two of these areas, but only when all three are combined can we enjoy a well-balanced life, a life of resounding victory. Those who cultivate such all-around strength are never defeated. (2/2/93)

No matter what happens, please continue to chant daimoku—in both good times and bad, unswayed by joys or sorrows, happiness or suffering. Then you will be able to seize victory in daily life and in society. (2/14/90)

In Buddhism, we either win or lose—there is no middle ground. Now and in the future, let us advance, determined to win in every sphere of our lives. By winning in our lives, we advance kosen-rufu; and by advancing kosen-rufu, we win in our lives. (6/16/97)

Winning in life is not a matter of form or appearances. It has nothing to do with vanity. Victory in life ultimately hinges on whether one has truly fought, on whether one has truly advanced. (10/25/96)

Winning in the end is what matters. The wins and losses along the way are of secondary significance. It's final victory in life that counts and that is the reason for our Buddhist practice. No matter how powerful, famous or privileged a person might be, Nichiren Daishonin says it is all nothing more than a dream, an illusory pleasure. True happiness can be attained only by revealing the state of Buddhahood within our lives. (3/5/97)

Buddhism concerns itself with winning. When we battle a powerful enemy, either we will triumph or we will be defeated — there is no middle ground. Battling against life's negative functions is an integral part of Buddhism. It is through victory in this struggle over negative forces that we become Buddhas. We must win. Moreover, Buddhism ensures that we can definitely do so. (3/24/97)

The important thing is to advance brightly, to strive for victory each moment, right where we are; to begin something here and now instead of fretting and worrying over what might happen. This is the starting point for transforming our lives. (3/8/96)

The British essayist William Hazlitt (1778–1830) was an acute observer of human psychology. He wrote that if we believe we can win, we will, asserting that confidence is a prerequisite for victory. The belief that you will win without fail summons all your strength, even that which is normally latent, making your triumph a reality. (3/9/93)

When you clearly envision a victorious outcome, engrave it in your heart and are firmly convinced that you will attain it, your brain makes every effort to realize the mental image you have created. Then, through unceasing efforts, that victory is finally made reality. You are the playwright of your own victory. (3/9/93)

Among other things, the great French general Napoleon Bonaparte (1769–1821) is famous for the remark "You write to me that it's impossible; the word is not French." Napoleon was not boasting of his great deeds, saying "Nothing is impossible for me." Rather, he was saying that it was precisely because he so firmly believed that nothing was impossible for human beings that he had achieved great accomplishments. (3/9/93)

Strength is happiness. Strength is itself victory. In weakness or cowardice there is no happiness. When you wage a struggle, you might win or lose. But regardless of the short-term outcome, the very fact that you continue to struggle proves your victory as a human being. A strong spirit, strong faith and strong prayer—developing these is victory and the world of Buddhahood. (10/25/96)

Faith enables us to secure ultimate victory. It enables us to live with vigor and joy and to strive to improve ourselves—to become the very best people we can be. Moreover, faith enables us to walk through life with complete assurance and confidence, afraid of nothing. (2/21/98)

Strength is the source of happiness. We mustn't shy away from life's challenges. We mustn't be defeated. Refusing defeat equals victory. A person who perseveres until the end is a winner. In the course of promoting our movement, the Soka Gakkai has never pulled back in the face of any challenge. We have kept moving forward, and that is the key to our success. Never to retreat a single step, no matter what—that is the Soka Gakkai spirit. Those who embrace this spirit can achieve unlimited victory. (3/8/98)

Buddhism stresses the importance of being victorious. Life, too, is a struggle for victory. Chanting daimoku is fundamental to victory. Nothing can match the power of daimoku. As long as we persevere in chanting daimoku, we have nothing to fear. (1/6/96)

The efforts made by one individual can be immensely important. Nichiren Daishonin repeatedly states that victory depends not on numbers but on a group or individual's attitude and resolve. In one passage he writes: "Everyone in Japan, from the sovereign on down to the common people, all without exception tried to do me harm, but I have survived until this day. This is because, although I am alone, I have firm faith [in the Lotus Sutra]" (MW-3, 198). In other words, his strong faith enabled him to emerge triumphant. I find this passage deeply moving. (1/8/98)

The sun rises every day. On cloudy days, stormy days, winter or summer, the sun is always shining. This is a law of the universe. No one can deny that truth. We, too, must live each day of our lives to the fullest. It makes sense that we do so. Victory belongs to those who persevere tenaciously in living fully. (DOY 1, ch. 2)

WOMEN

The conversation of women of keen perception who are sensitive to the feelings of others has the power to open even the most heavily barricaded heart. It is invariably women's cries for justice that move people to action and change the times. (1/31/93)

Nichiren Daishonin clearly teaches, "There should be no discrimination among those who propagate the five characters of Myoho-renge-kyo in the Latter Day of the Law, be they men or women" (MW-1, 93). The equality and equal rights of men and women lie at the very core of Buddhist teachings. This is something that will never change. (1/27/96)

∿

Emerson held great expectations for women in society: "Women are, by this [their power of conversation] and their social influence, the civilizers of humankind. What is civilization? I answer, the power of good women." These are my sentiments exactly. "Good women," as he puts it, are the bastions of civilization and culture. (1/6/96)

∿

The Soka Gakkai has developed in large part thanks to the efforts of the women's division members. I hope that women will always be accorded the highest respect. (1/6/96)

∿

Where can we find real proof of the greatness of the Mystic Law? In "The Daimoku of the Lotus Sutra," the Daishonin reveals that the Lotus Sutra's teaching of enlightenment for women provides one example of such proof. The Lotus Sutra accords the highest respect to women—who in earlier teachings had been spurned and unjustly discriminated against — making it possible for them to lead supremely noble lives and seize personal victory. (1/6/96)

∿

I would like the members of the women's division, in particular, to become experts in happiness and daily life. Steering your families on a course toward happiness like so many accomplished pilots, please become the radiant "flowers" and "suns" of the SGI. (1/27/96)

I hope that all of you women will be cultured and graceful. Intelligent and kind people are beautiful. They inspire trust and a sense of reassurance in those around them. As you continue to deepen your faith in Buddhism, you can broaden your sphere of knowledge. (2/27/90)

I hope that the members of the women's division learn the correct way to practice Buddhism, so that if a leader or a male does something that goes against reason, you will be able to clearly point out the error and identify the correct path or the correct standard for them to follow. Nichiren Daishonin compares men to an arrow and women to the bow. An arrow flies in the direction that the bow points it. (2/27/90)

I would like to tell you that when the members of the women's division freely devote themselves to activities and provide a confident, strong lead for the men, that will mark the dawn of the new "SGI-USA." (2/27/90)

The Daishonin praised the mother of Oto Gozen, saying, "You are undoubtedly the foremost votary of the Lotus Sutra among the women of Japan" (MW-3, 52). And he gave her the name Nichimyo Shonin. *Nichi* is from Nichiren, meaning sun, and *myo* is the first part of *myoho*, or Mystic Law. He adds the honorific title *Shonin*, meaning sage or saint. We see that distinctions between priesthood and laity, male and female, did not matter in the least to Nichiren Daishonin; he fixed his gaze solely on people's hearts or their spirit. (LG, p. 128)

In his guidance to the wives of the Ikegami brothers, Nichiren Daishonin states, "If both of you unite in encouraging their (your husbands') faith, you will follow the path of the Dragon King's daughter and become the model for women attaining enlightenment in the evil Latter Day of the Law" (MW-1, 146). This passage reflects the Daishonin's strict yet compassionate advice to his female followers. I hope that you will take it deeply to heart. (2/21/90)

YOUTH

Youth is a truly wonderful thing. Unfortunately though, this is often something that's hard to appreciate when we're young. Life passes by quickly. Before we know it, we are old. That's why in our youth we should be as active as we possibly can. Rather than a life of blank pages, live a life crammed full of memories—of battles well fought and wonderfully diverse experiences. Not to leave behind any history, just to grow old and die, is a sad way to live. (5/26/98)

The stronger the oppression from without, the stronger one's determination to summon forth one's inner resources to fight against it—this is the spirit of youth. (7/19/96)

Youth must have the spirit to attack injustice, the spirit to refute what is wrong, the spirit to spread the Daishonin's teaching. Just giving the appearance of promoting kosen-rufu, "going with the flow," afraid of "making waves," are the actions of self-serving youth who are already spiritually old and decrepit. (3/13/98)

Youth means to cherish hope; it is a time of development. Youth means to challenge oneself; it is a time of construction. Youth means to fight for justice; it is a time of action. (8/18/96)

Youth, and indeed life itself, flashes by in the blink of an eye. That is why it is important for you to ask yourselves what you can do for those who are suffering, what you can do to resolve the mournful contradictions that plague society, and to boldly take on these great challenges without shunning the subsequent problems and difficulties you will inevitably face. (4/2/96)

Youth should not seek an easy, comfortable path. No one develops in a pampered environment. Youth should instead actively seek out challenges and hardships, transforming them all into valuable assets as they strive to become individuals of outstanding character and ability. (7/19/96)

Youth is a season of unrest and agony. This is true of young people all over the world. In a sense, it may all be for the best. You are certainly not suffering on your own; and since young people are all experiencing change and growth, such feelings are only natural. (2/26/90)

Life is like a marathon, as is faith. Though you may lose the lead in the midst of the race, victory or defeat is decided at the finish line. Your training during youth is to enable you to win ultimate and true victory. Therefore, now is the time when you must study as much as you can and chant abundant daimoku so that you can greatly increase your life force for life's marathon. (2/26/90)

Life is long. The true result of your daily struggles will be revealed in your 40s, 50s and 60s. So it is important that you each find something—it doesn't matter what—with which to challenge yourselves while you are young. Regard your youth as the time to study and train yourselves. (DOY 1, ch. 8)

President Toda once said, "It is vital for youth to have the tenacity to become the very best at something." Tenacity is crucial. You cannot make the gem inside your life shine with easygoing efforts. (DOY 1, ch. 8)

Nothing can equal the splendor of youth. To be young is to possess a treasure of infinite worth far greater than any person of power. This is all the more true of you who possess the eternal treasure of the Mystic Law. Those who live based on this supreme Law are bodhisattvas and Buddhas. (5/8/98)

YOUTHFUL SPIRIT

Our Buddhist practice enables us to firmly establish a life-condition of perennial youth forged through overcoming various trials in life. This is called "never aging" or "perpetual youth." We begin to grow old from the moment we lose hope and the spirit of challenge, when we become self-satisfied or grow resigned to our present circumstances. (5/17/91)

Buddhism teaches that immense blessings accrue to a single moment of rejoicing on hearing the Lotus Sutra. A mind that is moved by and rejoices at the greatness of the Mystic Law is itself the key to eternal youth. (3/8/96)

The German author Hermann Hesse (1877–1962) writes that the more one matures, the younger one grows. Certainly there are many people who as they age become increasingly vigorous and energetic, more broad-minded and tolerant, living with a greater sense of freedom and assurance. It is important to remember that aging and growing old are not necessarily the same. (1/8/98)

What is youth? The French philosopher Roger Garaudy suggests that while most people believe a person is born young, then ages and dies, in reality, acquiring youth in the deepest sense is a very long and challenging process. The youth of which he speaks is the spiritual strength not to stagnate or grow resistant to change but to stay open to new possibilities. It is a power of spirit that refuses to succumb to complacency and strives forward. (1/8/98)

You mustn't allow yourselves to grow old before your time. Please live with a youthful spirit. That is what Buddhism teaches us to do and it is how life should be lived. If you make a commitment to work for the sake of others, you will be rejuvenated. If you devote your life to helping others, you'll stay young. The power of Nam-myoho-renge-kyo guarantees this. (6/16/98)

Faith and Practice

ACTION

Buddhism means putting the teachings into practice. Practice equals faith. With a practice of sincere prayer and action, our desires cannot possibly fail to be fulfilled. When you continue to apply yourselves to your Buddhist practice toward kosen-rufu, solidifying and gaining mastery in faith, all your prayers will definitely be answered. (1/27/93)

When we take action, new possibilities are created and fresh impetus is given to our endeavors. This is how we can expand our network of friends. More than mere words or appearances, what is essential to this expansion are concrete actions. (2/25/96)

Prayer is not a feeble consolation; it is a powerful, unyielding conviction. And prayer must become manifest in action. To put it another way, if our prayers are in earnest, they will definitely give rise to action. (LG, p. 93)

Prayer becomes manifest in action, and action has to be backed up by prayer. Only then can we elicit a response from the Buddhist deities and all Buddhas. Those who pray and take action for kosen-rufu are the Buddha's emissaries. They cannot fail to realize lives in which all desires are fulfilled. (LG, p. 93)

Gandhi declared, "Unwearied, ceaseless effort is the price that must be paid for turning faith into a rich infallible experience." In the final analysis, faith that is not accompanied by action is mere abstraction. Ceaseless effort is what makes our faith a living and breathing part of us. Making our faith in the Daishonin's Buddhism an active and indivisible part of our lives is what it means to attain Buddhahood. (6/1/96)

I always place a high value on personal initiative. Spontaneity underlies the spirit of autonomy and independence; conversely, taking action because one is told to amounts to slavery of the spirit. (2/14/90)

Buddhism holds that everything is in a constant state of flux. Thus the question is whether we accept change passively and are swept away by it or whether we take the lead and create positive changes on our own initiative. While conservatism and self-protection might be likened to winter, night and death, the spirit of pioneering and attempting to realize ideals evoke images of spring, morning and birth. (2/21/90)

Prayer is the foundation. But at the same time if we fail to make concrete efforts, no matter how much daimoku we chant, our prayers will not be answered. Buddhism is reason. If we just chant without doing any work, we cannot succeed in our jobs. (6/5/96)

The Gohonzon is the physical manifestation of the very existence of Nichiren Daishonin, who taught kosen-rufu. Because of this, if you only practice gongyo and chant daimoku and don't take any other action for the sake of kosen-rufu or improving your own life, the Gohonzon will not have its true, full effect. If, however, you take actions to achieve kosen-rufu, those actions will serve as that extra push for your own life, helping you leap to higher and higher states of mind in your gongyo and chanting. (2/19/90)

One meaning of *kyo* of Nam-myoho-renge-kyo is action. Without action, we cannot say that we are practicing Nam-myoho-renge-kyo; it would remain a mere concept. Only through action can we truly gain the great benefit of the Mystic Law. (4/23/96)

"What kinds of causes am I making right now?" "What actions am I taking?" The answers to these questions are what will determine our future—in this life and throughout the three existences. Herein lies the foundation of faith. True glory and victory in life lie in basing oneself on this fundamental principle. (10/25/96)

It's all about taking action, taking that first step. If your aim is to swim across a vast ocean, it will do you no good to get cold feet before you even take the plunge. Rather, you've got to make a move, keeping your sights on your distant goal. Hindsight can be valuable toward one's growth, but it is self-defeating to set oneself up for failure before even trying. (DOY 1, ch. 10)

BENEFIT

We are a gathering of the Buddha's children. Therefore, if we respect one another, our good fortune will multiply infinitely, like an image reflected between mirrors. A person who practices alone cannot experience this tremendous multiplication of benefit. (2/27/90)

The real benefit of the Mystic Law is of an inconspicuous kind. Just as trees grow taller and stronger year after year, adding growth rings imperceptible to the human eye, we, too, will grow to have a victorious existence. For this reason, it is important that we lead tenacious and balanced lives based on faith. (6/5/96)

Nothing is wasted in faith. One never loses out. Please be confident that all your efforts to help others and promote Buddhism are accumulating immense treasures of good fortune in your life. This is what is meant by inconspicuous benefit. (5/26/98)

If somewhere in your heart you have decided "I alone am incapable of becoming happy," "Only I cannot become a capable person" or "Only my sufferings will forever remain unresolved" then that factor in your mind or determination will obstruct your benefit. (LG, p. 240)

The second Soka Gakkai president, Josei Toda, often used to cite fifteen years as the first milestone for showing actual proof in faith. He would say that even a small bud grows into a great tree after fifteen years. Someone who had not seen the bud sprout and grow during those fifteen years would be amazed by its growth; this is what is called an inconspicuous benefit. On the

other hand, he observed, a great tree may also wither away during a fifteen-year period; this is an example of inconspicuous
punishment or loss. (6/15/96)

Daily life is a collection of both good things (value) and bad
things (antivalue). If the value or benefit in someone's life out-
weighs the antivalue or loss, the person becomes happy. If the
opposite is true, the person is unhappy. (LG, p. 105)

Faith in the Mystic Law is the wellspring of value creation. It enables us to turn everything in our lives—both our joys and sufferings—into causes for accumulating beauty, benefit and good
in still greater measure. When we base ourselves on this kind of
faith, everything that happens to us is a benefit. (LG, p. 104)

There are two kinds of benefit that derive from faith in the
Gohonzon: conspicuous and inconspicuous. Conspicuous
benefit is the obvious, visible benefit of being protected or
being quickly able to surmount a problem when it arises, be
it an illness or a conflict in personal relationships. Inconspicuous benefit is good fortune accumulated slowly but steadily, like the growth of a tree or the rising of the tide, which
results in the forging of a rich and expansive state of life. We
might not discern any change from day to day, but as the
years pass, it will be clear that we've become happy, that we've
grown as individuals. (DOY 2, ch. 20)

No matter what happens, the important thing is to continue
chanting. If you do so, you'll definitely become happy. Even
if things don't work out the way you had hoped or imagined,
when you look back later, you'll understand, on a much more

profound level, that it was in fact the best possible result. This is the way of tremendous inconspicuous benefit. (DOY 2, ch. 20)

BODHISATTVA SPIRIT

As Buddhists, our greatest hope is happiness not only for ourselves and those near and dear to us but also for our friends and fellow members. "I want so-and-so to become happy. I want to enable all the members to enjoy themselves" — there is no more lofty way of life than praying for and exerting ourselves for others' happiness. (9/26/93)

"So-and-so is sick. So-and-so is suffering financially. I must do my best to give them encouragement." To think in this way, to offer prayers and take action for others' happiness — this is the behavior of a true Buddhist. (9/18/93)

The following three traits summarize the character and mentality of the Bodhisattvas of the Earth:
- To be rigorously strict toward oneself, like a sharp autumn frost.
- To be warm and embracing toward others, like a soft spring breeze.
- To be uncompromising when confronting evil, like a lion monarch. (1999 PP)

Where outside of the SGI can we find a group of people who pray and take action for the sake of others and society while enduring attacks and persecutions? Our organization is indeed a gathering of bodhisattvas. Such altruistic actions are surely beyond the ability of any but the Bodhisattvas of the Earth. (Dialogue 1, 1994)

~

Suffering and undergoing hardships for the sake of friends and for the sake of spreading the Law is a manifestation of a bodhisattva's behavior and a genuine leader's great sense of responsibility. There is no suffering or hardship that a Bodhisattva of the Earth cannot surmount. So no matter what happens, I would like you to steadily advance, one step at a time, always chanting Nam-myoho-renge-kyo with vibrant voices. (6/15/96)

~

Buddhism is not about leading a self-centered existence. If we do not base our lives on the Law, we are not practicing Buddhism. The German writer Friedrich von Schiller writes, "The brave man thinks upon himself the last." This is analogous to the spirit of not begrudging one's life taught in the Lotus Sutra. This means treasuring the Law more highly than one's life. The Law and kosen-rufu are central to one's life. (2/3/98)

~

You must have self-discipline. And that comes from chanting daimoku, from developing a strong life force. When you bring forth your Buddhahood, your passionate nature will become your impetus for progress, a strong sense of justice and a burning desire to help other people. (DOY 1, ch. 10)

~

Nichiren Daishonin writes, "If you light a lantern for another, it will also brighten your own way" (*Gosho Zenshu*, p. 1598). Please be confident that the higher your flame of altruistic action burns, the more its light will suffuse your life with happiness. Those who possess an altruistic spirit are the happiest people of all. (1/31/93)

Bodhisattvas are courageous individuals who plunge head-long into the thick of society to lead others to happiness. What kind of character should bodhisattvas possess? Shakya-muni asserts that they should have hearts invulnerable to as-saults from the eight winds. (3/3/96)

Today's world is sorely lacking in hope, a positive vision for the future and a solid philosophy. There is no bright light il-luminating the horizon. That is precisely why we, the Bodhi-sattvas of the Earth, have appeared. That is why Nichiren Daishonin's Buddhism of the sun is so essential. We have stood up, holding high the torch of courage in one hand and the philosophy of truth and justice in the other. We have be-gun to take action to boldly break through the darkness of the four sufferings of birth, old age, sickness and death as well as the darkness in society and the world. (6/15/96)

Today's world is sorely lacking in hope, a positive vision for the future and a solid philosophy. There is no bright light il-luminating the horizon. That is precisely why we, the Bodhi-sattvas of the Earth, have appeared. That is why Nichiren Daishonin's Buddhism of the sun is so essential. We have stood up, holding high the torch of courage in one hand and the philosophy of truth and justice in the other. We have be-gun to take action to boldly break through the darkness of the four sufferings of birth, old age, sickness and death as well as the darkness in society and the world. (6/15/96)

In this Latter Day of the Law teeming with perverse individ-uals, you are exerting yourselves energetically, often amid many hardships and obstacles, chanting daimoku for the sake of others' happiness, traveling long distances to meet with friends, to talk with them and show them warm concern and understanding. You are truly bodhisattvas; there is no more noble life, no life based on a more lofty philosophy. (6/23/96)

BUDDHA AND BUDDHAHOOD

Nichiren Daishonin urges that we make our lives shine with "the serene light of the moon of enlightenment" (*Gosho Zenshu,* p. 1262). This refers to the enlightenment of Buddhahood. When the light of the moon breaks through the clouds, in an instant the darkness of night is dispelled. The full moon brilliantly illuminates both the heavens and the earth below. Similarly, when the world of Buddhahood shines from the depths of our lives, the clouds of anguish are dispelled. (Dialogue 1, 1994)

The world of Buddhahood expressed by Nam-myoho-renge-kyo exists within our lives. To die without having glimpsed this state of life is most pitiful. If we truly treasure our lives, then it is vital that we contact the Buddha within. (Dialogue 1, 1994)

What does attaining Buddhahood mean for us? It does not mean that one day we suddenly turn into a Buddha or become magically enlightened. Someone who claims the latter is more than likely a fraud. In a sense, attaining Buddhahood means that we have securely entered the path, or orbit, of Buddhahood. (3/8/96)

Rather than a final, static destination at which we arrive and remain, achieving enlightenment means firmly establishing the faith needed to keep advancing along the path of absolute happiness limitlessly, endlessly. (3/8/96)

The glory we enjoy in a dream vanishes without a trace when we awake. When an illusion disappears, nothing is left of its joy, only a sense of emptiness like that one feels when sobering from a state of drunkenness. The joy of Buddhahood, however, is profound, indestructible and everlasting. (3/9/96)

Once we awaken to our Buddha nature, we need not be grieved any longer. Our lives are filled with the greatest of joys. A world of infinite joy blossoms in our daily lives. It is our mission to teach this to others; thus, friends of the Mystic Law are ambassadors of joy. (2/26/90)

While controlling your mind, which is at once both extremely subtle and solemnly profound, you should strive to elevate your faith with freshness and vigor. When you do so, both your life and your surroundings will open wide before you, and every action you take will become a source of benefit. Understanding the subtle workings of one's mind is the key to faith and to attaining Buddhahood in this lifetime. (2/27/90)

The Daishonin says, "Even common mortals can attain Buddhahood if they cherish one thing: earnest faith" (MW-1, 268). We need to direct our spirit, our hearts, toward kosen-rufu. Attaining Buddhahood depends on cherishing this resolve. When we have such a spirit, our lives sparkle with jewels of good fortune and happiness. We undertake a wonderful journey through life in which our dreams, one after another, are accomplished. (LG, p. 131)

President Toda said: "While people today are extremely greedy, they do not desire the vast benefit of attaining Buddhahood. On this point they could be called unselfish, people of modest wants, or just plain foolish." With "great greed for attaining Buddhahood," let us continue working to develop the state of life of absolute happiness in our own lives—the state in which life itself is an irrepressible joy—while enabling friends to do the same. (LG, p. 81)

We can attain a happy life state that shines like a diamond, solemn and indestructible under all circumstances. And we can do so in this lifetime. The Lotus Sutra exists to enable all people to attain such a state of life. (LG, p. 42)

The Daishonin described his daily existence in the frankest terms. If it were cold, he would say it was cold. If he were suffering from hunger, he would indicate it. A Buddha is not some special being. A Buddha is human through and through. (LG, p. 22)

President Toda often called the Daishonin a "great common mortal." And he hated being referred to, with bated breath, as "the founder." Buddhism is not a religion that produces so-called living Buddhas. Rather, it enables ordinary people, just as they are, to manifest the light of supreme humanity. (LG, p. 22)

If we attain the state of Buddhahood in this lifetime, that state will forever pervade our lives. This state of life is everlasting. It can never be destroyed. It is precisely so that you may enjoy such eternal happiness that I continually urge you to apply yourself to your Buddhist practice and firmly consolidate the state of Buddhahood in your life in this existence. This is not just a matter of personal sentiment; it is the teaching of Nichiren Daishonin. (6/15/96)

～

In the "Ongi Kuden" (Record of the Orally Transmitted Teachings), Nichiren Daishonin says with reference to attaining Buddhahood, "'To attain' means 'to open'" (*Gosho Zenshu*, p. 753). Attaining Buddhahood means opening our lives to their fullest potential and revealing our innate Buddhahood. This is the purpose of Buddhism. (1/28/93)

～

How can we create the greatest value in the short span of a lifetime? Those of us who embrace the Mystic Law know the answer. Our faith in and practice of the Daishonin's Buddhism enables us, in this lifetime, to solidify the world of Buddhahood in our lives and establish a state of eternal happiness. That is the purpose of faith in the Mystic Law and the purpose of our Buddhist practice. (9/26/96)

～

Your faith guarantees that an infinite number of your ancestors and descendants will attain Buddhahood. Such is the wondrous power of the Mystic Law. How profound and important is your existence! There is also no greater way to repay the debt of gratitude owed to your parents than through faith. (3/20/96)

～

Worldly success and good circumstances based on luck can easily crumble. They are as transient as an illusion. But the state of Buddhahood, once attained, can never be destroyed, not for eternity. We will enjoy existences overflowing with good fortune and immense joy in lifetime after lifetime. (5/23/96)

CAUSE AND EFFECT

Though cosmetics can be applied to the face, we cannot gloss over the face of our soul. The law of cause and effect functioning in the depths of life is strict and impartial. (2/27/90)

Benefit and loss are not imparted by someone else. When we act in accordance with the Law, value is produced. When we go against the Law, we receive retribution. To use a familiar example, if you go outside in the severe cold of winter without wearing warm clothes, you might experience the loss of becoming sick. Benefit produces value in life, whereas loss produces antivalue. (LG, p. 101)

Buddhism teaches that unseen virtue brings about visible reward. In the world of Buddhism, we never fail to receive an effect for our actions—whether for good or bad; therefore, it makes no sense to be two-faced or to put on airs. (2/27/90)

In the inner realm of life, cause and effect occur simultaneously. With the passage of time, this causal relationship becomes manifest in the phenomenal world of daily life. (2/27/90)

The people around us reflect our state of life. Our personal preferences, for example, are mirrored in their attitudes. This is especially clear from the viewpoint of Buddhism, which elucidates the workings of cause and effect as if in a spotless mirror. (2/27/90)

~

People who use their legs, who move around for the sake of Buddhism, gain the good fortune and benefit with which to freely travel the world. People who prepare places for Buddhist meetings, including those who clean the community and training centers, develop the state of life to dwell in "bejeweled houses" in the future. These examples are not fairy tales. The Mystic Law is wondrous and inscrutable. This is a function of the law of the simultaneity of cause and effect. (LG, p. 133)

~

Daimoku is like light. As the Daishonin says, "A candle can light up a place that has been dark for billions of years." Similarly, the moment we offer prayers based on daimoku, the darkness in our lives vanishes. This is the principle of the simultaneity of cause and effect. At that very instant in the depths of our lives our prayer has been answered. (LG, p. 88)

~

The inherent cause (*nyo ze in*) of a deep prayer simultaneously produces a latent effect (*nyo ze ka*). While it takes time for this effect to become manifest, our prayers are immediately realized in the depths of our lives. So at that moment light shines forth. The lotus flower (*renge*) in blooming and seeding at the same time illustrates this principle of simultaneity of cause and effect. (LG, p. 88)

~

There is a Russian proverb that says: "It is no use to blame the looking glass if your face is awry." Likewise, one's happiness or unhappiness is entirely the reflection of the balance of both good and bad causes accumulated in one's life. No one can blame others for his misfortunes. In the world of faith it is necessary to realize this clearly. (2/27/90)

The Daishonin explains the significance of cause and effect: All sutras other than the Lotus Sutra expound that Buddhahood (effect) can be attained only after having made good causes, that is, practicing their teachings (causes), over a length of time. With the Lotus Sutra, however, the very act of embracing it (cause) enables one simultaneously to become a Buddha (effect). (2/24/90)

What will the future be like? No one knows the answer to this question. All we know is that the effects that will appear in the future are all contained in the causes made in the present. The important thing, therefore, is that we stand up and take action to achieve great objectives without allowing ourselves to be distracted or discouraged by immediate difficulties. (5/17/97)

The law of causality guarantees that all your efforts will definitely adorn your future with blessings and good fortune. Please also be assured that your benefits will be passed down generation after generation to your descendants. (2/3/93)

CONVICTION

If you practice faith while doubting its effects, you will get results that are at best unsatisfactory. This is the reflection of your own weak faith in the mirror of the cosmos. On the other hand, when you stand up with strong confidence, you will accrue limitless blessings. (2/27/90)

I want to raise champions, genuine champions who will fight for the people with indomitable resolve. I want to foster champions who possess courage, champions who will defend freedom, who are warm human beings yet uncompromising when it comes to fighting evil. (Dialogue 13, 1994)

President Toda often said: "Those of you who have problems or sufferings, pray earnestly! Buddhism is a deadly serious win-or-lose struggle. If you should [pray with such an earnest attitude] and still have no solution forthcoming, then I will give you my life!" This invincible conviction, on which Mr. Toda was willing to stake his life, inspired the members. (1/27/93)

Without great confidence in one's own beliefs, it is impossible to help others or to lead them to happiness. Without unshakable conviction, it is impossible to endure suppression and to resist temptation. (Dialogue 13, 1994)

In one essay Emerson records these words: "The more trouble, the more lion; that's my principle." Just whose words were these? Emerson's own? Those of some famous philosopher? No, they were the words of a poor woman of no particular standing. Deeply impressed by her conviction, Emerson recorded her words and so gave her a place in history. (1/6/96)

The important thing is to hold on resolutely to one's convictions come what may, just as the Daishonin teaches. People who possess such unwavering conviction will definitely become happy. (6/23/96)

To lead a life in which we are inspired and can inspire others, our hearts have to be alive; they have to be filled with passion and enthusiasm. To achieve that, as President Toda said, we need the courage to "live true to ourselves." And to live true to ourselves, we need the strength of mind not to be swayed by our environment or be obsessed with superficial appearances. Rather than borrowing from or imitating others, we need the conviction to be able to think for ourselves and to take action out of our own sense of responsibility. (5/18/95)

Leo Tolstoy concluded that the only way to bring about a fundamental change in society is to realize a change in public opinion, a change in people's minds. Then how can we change public opinion? Tolstoy asserted: "It is necessary only for people to say what they really think or at least to refrain from saying what they do not think." It is vital, in other words, not to be swayed by others' opinions or past ways of thought or action. Instead each of us must become wise, possessing our own firm convictions. (1/29/95)

When you encounter a wall you should tell yourself, "Since there is a wall here, a wide open expanse must lie on the other side." Rather than becoming discouraged, know that encountering a wall is proof of the progress that you have made so far. I hope that you will continually advance in your

Buddhist practice with this conviction blazing ever more strongly in your heart. (3/28/95)

～

One's true worth as a human being is not a matter of outward appearance or title but derives from the breadth of one's spirit. Everything comes down to faith and conviction. It is what is in one's heart and the substance of one's actions that count. (8/29/96)

～

Faith is light. The hearts of those with strong faith are filled with light. A radiance envelops their lives. People with unshakable conviction in faith enjoy a happiness that is as luminous as the full moon on a dark night, as dazzling as the sun on a clear day. (6/5/96)

～

A voice that rings with deep conviction derived from faith in the Mystic Law functions as an instrument to carry out the Buddha's work, whether it be encouraging and praising others, engaging in dialogue, trying to impart understanding and peace of mind, or saying what has to be said. (1/31/93)

COURAGE

Cowardice is harmful, for it delights the enemies of Buddhism and obstructs the advance of kosen-rufu. The fainthearted cannot savor the true benefit of faith; their ability to tap the power of the Buddha and the power of the Law [of the Gohonzon] in their lives is feeble. (9/15/97)

～

We must have the spirit of a lion. The Daishonin says, "The lion fears no other beast" (MW-1, 241). Courage is the absolute condition for attaining Buddhahood. Courage is the absolute condition for becoming happy. (LG, p. 215)

We are direct followers of Nichiren Daishonin, a person of the greatest courage. We have to stand alone with the courage of lions. Like lions, we have to fight courageously to win the laurel wreath of victory. (LG, p. 215)

Courageous people can overcome anything. Cowardly people, on the other hand, because of their lack of courage, fail to savor the true, profound joys of life. This is truly unfortunate. (6/23/96)

Those who don't speak the truth when it is time to may avoid immediate danger. Those who don't take courageous action may live in peace and security temporarily. This is what wily and cunning people do. (LG, p. 195)

The important thing is to take that first step. Bravely overcoming one small fear gives you the courage to take on the next. (DOY 1, ch. 10)

Nichiren Daishonin teaches the spirit that "not to advance is to retreat." The point is to continue forging ahead despite any storms or hardships that may arise, to be fearless and advance like a lion. (10/25/96)

To be fearless no matter what happens—that is the root of true happiness. To move forward resolutely regardless of what lies in store—that is the spirit, the resolve, that leads to human victory. But if we allow ourselves to be disturbed by petty criticism and slander, if we fear pressure or persecution, we will never advance or create anything of lasting value. (4/23/96)

Kosen-rufu will be advanced by brave people armed with the spirit of independence who voluntarily strive to fulfill the vow they made at the time of *kuon ganjo*. Because they struggle of their own volition, they have no complaints or grievances. The greater the obstacles they face, the greater the courage, wisdom and power they muster from within. (2/14/90)

Great individuals fight abuses of authority. The truly strong do not lord it over the weak. People of genuine strength and courage battle against the powerful, the arrogant, the authoritarian, the evil and corrupt—all who look down on the people with contempt. (5/26/98)

Please never turn your back on your faith. Courage is crucial. There is no room for faintheartedness in faith. The timid doom themselves to ridicule from their partners, from their children, from their friends and from the world at large. The Daishonin declares that there is no place for cowards among his disciples. (4/20/98)

Life is full of unexpected suffering. Even so, as Eleanor Roosevelt said: "If you can live through that [a difficult situation]

you can live through anything. You gain strength, courage and confidence by every experience in which you really stop to look fear in the face. You are able to say to yourself, 'I lived through this horror. I can take the next thing that comes along.'" That's exactly right. Struggling against great difficulty enables us to develop ourselves tremendously. We then call forth and manifest those abilities dormant within us. Difficulty can then be a source of dynamic new growth and positive progress. (10/6/95).

In his later years, President Toda often told his disciples: "Be courageous in faith! No matter what other people may say, advance boldly! Lead confident lives! Make courage the Gakkai's eternal emblem!" This was the mission with which he charged us before he died. Faith is the source of true strength and courage. Without courage and confidence we cannot be said to have genuine faith. (2/3/98)

In 1912, at the time of the tragic sinking of the *Titanic*, Molly Brown, a native of Denver, was on board. Although she knew the ship was taking on water, she shouted to a panic-stricken fellow passenger: "There's no danger. It simply can't go down, because I'm on it and I'm unsinkable." Her bantering words, which rang out with a determination to never be defeated and to never give in to despair, are said to have given courage to fellow passengers as she assisted them into the lifeboats. Those who stand up at a crucial moment demonstrate genuine greatness. They are people who leave an immortal history. (6/10/96)

DETERMINATION

Even one daimoku can permeate the entire universe. How much greater then is daimoku's capacity to move anything when it is chanted with sincerity and determination! Daimoku chanted with the profound conviction that "my life is the entity of the Mystic Law" or with the resolve that "I will dedicate my life to spreading the Mystic Law as an emissary of the Buddha" cannot fail to draw a response from the Gohonzon. Such daimoku cannot fail to permeate the universe. (7/21/92)

Invisible radio waves travel vast distances through space, reaching Mars and Venus. In the same way, our inner determination, which is unobservable to common mortals, activates the forces in the universe—the heavenly deities and the Buddhas throughout the ten directions—and appears as solid actual proof in accordance with the principle of 3,000 realms in a single moment of life. (4/11/92)

Faith means making 100 percent effort—in our daimoku and in our actions. When we practice in this way, the Buddhist gods will lend us their protection. We mustn't have a complacent, dependent attitude in faith, chanting haphazardly without definite goals, making only halfhearted efforts in the belief that we'll be protected automatically. Deep determination and unshakable character are vital. Those with these qualities are second to none in faith. (11/25/96)

When your determination changes, everything will begin to move in the direction you desire. The moment you resolve to be victorious, every nerve and fiber in your being will immediately orient itself toward your success. On the other hand, if you think, "This is never going to work out," then at that instant every cell in your being will be deflated and give up the fight. Then everything really will move in the direction of failure. (3/24/97)

Anyone who has ever made a resolution discovers that the strength of that determination fades in time. The moment you feel that is when you should make a fresh determination. Tell yourselves: "OK! I will start again from now!" If you fall down seven times, get up the eighth. Don't give up when you feel discouraged—just pick yourselves up and renew your determination each time. (DOY 1, ch. 6)

Life is a struggle with ourselves. It is a tug-of-war between progress and regression, between happiness and unhappiness. Those short on willpower or self-motivation should chant daimoku with conviction to become people of strong will who can tackle any problem with seriousness and determination. (DOY 1, ch. 6)

FAITH

What is the purpose of faith? It is so that each of us can become truly happy and enable others to become happy. Faith is the driving force that lets us apply what we gain from our studies to truly serving people. (DOY 2, ch. 19)

Faith is an issue of fundamental importance to us all. You can become genuine successors of the Soka Gakkai or great leaders for the twenty-first century only by establishing in your lives a firm foundation of strong, unshakable faith. (DOY 2, ch. 19)

People who have strong faith are fearless; they can overcome anything. There is no obstacle or adversity that they cannot surmount. In the very depths of their lives, no matter what happens, they lead lives of "the greatest of all joys." (6/10/96)

Faith is the most powerful force in the world. Many people put on a show of strength, but true strength has nothing to do with appearances. On the contrary, we usually find that the weaker the individual, the greater their bravado or outward display of strength. (5/26/98)

Everything is contained in the word *faith*. It encompasses truth, courage, wisdom and good fortune. It includes compassion and humanity, as well as peace, culture and happiness. (DOY 2, ch. 19)

Faith is eternal hope; it is the secret to limitless self-development. Faith is the most basic principle for growth. (DOY 2, ch. 19)

FORTUNE

Governments come and go, economies rise and fall, and society changes constantly. Only the good fortune we accumulate during our lives lasts forever. True victors are those who cultivate the tree of Buddhahood in the vast earth of their lives while achieving success both in society and in their personal lives through true faith and a true way of living. (3/9/96)

~

What is the secret to victory? Mr. Toda once described that, in a certain sense, life is a gamble. "If you are lucky, you will win," he said. "But if you are unlucky, then sometimes, no matter how hard you try, you lose. This is a hard fact." This is why, in addition to ability, good fortune is essential. The key to creating good fortune is found in faith and daimoku. I hope that you will all act in accord with the fundamental Law of Buddhism and lead victorious lives filled with unsurpassed good fortune. (2/17/96)

~

When we base our lives on the great wish for kosen-rufu, regarding each effort "like dew entering the ocean, or soil being added to the earth," then our petty lesser selves give way to the greater self that shines with eternal victory. Our every effort turns into an ocean of benefit, an earth of good fortune. (LG, p. 152)

~

The good fortune and benefit we create by exerting ourselves in faith will definitely manifest themselves in the lives of our children, grandchildren and all our family. Buddhism is the supreme medicine. The Daishonin says that the benefit of faith extends to the "preceding seven generations and the seven generations that followed" (MW-7, 172). (LG, p. 139)

~

Each one of you is translating our unsurpassed philosophy into action and spreading its message far and wide. To possess a philosophy of such profound value is, itself, the greatest good fortune. (6/23/96)

Viewed in light of the causal law of Buddhism, the great good fortune you are now accumulating in looking after and treasuring many people predestines you to a state of being where you will be supported and protected by many people in successive lifetimes. Our Buddhist practice in this life is our training for becoming great leaders throughout all future existences. (6/23/96)

Walt Whitman sings, "Henceforth I ask not good-fortune, I myself am good-fortune." Good fortune does not lie far away. Our lives themselves are entities of good fortune, entities of happiness, indestructible as diamonds. (LG, p. 47)

You erase good fortune when you allow yourself to become discouraged over, for example, losing an argument with your spouse. However, when you resolve to challenge the situation by chanting daimoku, you add a hefty increase to your accumulated store of fortune. The sum of these gains and losses represents the final balance of your happiness. (1/31/93)

GOHONZON

Specifically, it is the Gohonzon—the actual embodiment of the principle of 3,000 realms in a single moment of life—that enables all people to become Buddhas. When we actively base our lives on the Gohonzon, wisdom and vitality well forth and we enter a rhythm of total and complete victory. (LG, p. 42)

Observing one's mind means to perceive that one's life contains the ten worlds, and in particular, the world of Buddhahood. It was to enable people to realize this that Nichiren Daishonin bestowed the Gohonzon of "observing one's mind" upon all humankind. (2/27/90)

Just as you look into a mirror when you make up your face, to beautify "the face of the soul," you need a mirror that reflects the depths of your life. This mirror is none other than the Gohonzon of "observing one's mind" or, more precisely, observing one's life. (2/27/90)

The Gohonzon is the clearest of all mirrors, which reflects the entire universe exactly as it is. When you chant to the Gohonzon, you can perceive the true entity of your life and can tap the inexhaustible life force of Buddhahood. (2/27/90)

The eyes are indeed the window of the soul. The eyes express a person's life totally. Similarly, the immense energy of a nuclear explosion is expressed by the succinct formula $E=mc^2$. While these are merely analogies, the single phrase Nam-myoho-renge-kyo is the key that unlocks the limitless energy of life. The Gohonzon of Nam-myoho-renge-kyo contains all the wisdom of Buddhism and the Lotus Sutra. (LG, p. 79)

Josei Toda once said: "The Gohonzon is truly great. But because this is so simple, people fail to understand it." Because the Law is profound, its practice is simple. The more technology advances, machines become simpler to operate. Mr. Toda went so far as to liken the Gohonzon to a "happiness-manufacturing machine." And the switch for turning this machine on is chanting daimoku for oneself and others. It could be said that Nichiren Daishonin distilled Buddhism down to irreducible simplicity for all people. (LG, p. 79)

The eternal life of the universe exists within each of us. The Gohonzon resides within each of us. The Daishonin's Buddhism is a philosophy of utmost respect for human beings and for life. Nichiren Daishonin embodied the essence of his own life in the form of the Gohonzon to make it possible for us to summon forth the Gohonzon within our lives. (DOY 2, ch. 20)

Mirrors, which function by virtue of the laws of light and reflection, are a product of human wisdom. On the other hand, the Gohonzon, based on the Law of the universe and of life itself, is the culmination of the Buddha's wisdom and makes it possible for us to attain Buddhahood by providing us with a means of perceiving the true nature of our lives. (1/27/90)

GONGYO AND DAIMOKU

Buddhism aims to make people free in the most profound sense; its purpose is not to restrict or constrain. Doing gongyo is a right, not an obligation. Because Buddhism entails practice, tenacious efforts are required, but these are all for your own sake. If you want to have great benefits or develop a profound state of life, you should exert yourself accordingly. (2/25/90)

In a sense, there is no simpler Buddhist practice than doing gongyo and chanting daimoku. We do not have to undertake strange austerities, as in some esoteric Buddhist traditions. The very superiority of the Daishonin's Buddhism enables us to tap the state of Buddhahood through this very simple practice. (DOY 2, ch. 20)

If we don't practice gongyo, the rhythm of our lives will be thrown off kilter, just as a machine that isn't oiled will rust. Gongyo and chanting daimoku are like starting an automobile's engine every day and driving in the direction of happiness and truth. By doing so day after day, you will gradually attain perfect unity with the universe and the Law, the state of the Buddha. (2/19/90)

On some occasions, you may be unable to do gongyo or you may be able to only recite the *Hoben* and *Juryo* portions of the sutra book or just chant daimoku. Nevertheless, so long as you maintain faith you will not experience negative effects on account of your occasional failure to carry out a complete practice of gongyo. While you should not take advantage of this statement or misconstrue it as condoning a lax or lazy attitude, you do not have to be overly strict or inflexible in your practice. (2/25/90)

Gongyo and daimoku might be compared to the food that sustains our lives. Chanting daimoku corresponds to the main dish and doing gongyo to the side dishes. Like the main and side dishes of a meal, the two are complementary, and we need both to derive maximum joy from our practice. By taking such balanced "meals" every morning and evening, you can activate your inherent Buddha nature and eventually establish that as your fundamental state of life. (2/25/90)

Originally, every person's life is a brilliantly shining mirror. Differences become apparent depending on whether one polishes this mirror. A polished mirror is the Buddha's life, whereas a tarnished mirror is that of a common mortal. Chanting Nam-myoho-renge-kyo polishes our lives. (2/27/90)

Gongyo is a practice that calls forth and activates the infinite power the microcosm inherently possesses. It transforms your fate, breaks through any apparent dead end and converts sufferings into happiness. It creates a transformation, a revolution of the microcosm. It is a diagram in miniature of kosen-rufu in our lives. (2/19/90)

Chanting daimoku is a teaching that is "easy to embrace and easy to practice." Anyone can do it. It can be done anytime, anywhere. It is the most highly refined yet simplified method of Buddhist practice. As such, it is the perfect Buddhist teaching for not only the twenty-first century but for the twenty-second, thirtieth and fiftieth centuries, and for the 10,000 years and more of the Latter Day of the Law—in fact, for all eternity. (LG, p. 87)

The language of gongyo, of chanting daimoku, reaches the Gohonzon and the realms of the Buddhas and bodhisattvas of the three existences and the ten directions. That's why the voice of gongyo and daimoku directed to the Gohonzon, whether we understand it or not, reaches all the Buddhas, bodhisattvas and heavenly deities. They hear it and say, "Excellent, excellent!" in response, rejoicing and praising us, and the entire universe envelops us in light. (2/19/90)

President Toda, smiling brightly, would say: "If a large hospital were to concoct a treatment you took every day for an hour that would enable you to become happy without fail in both body and spirit, the place would no doubt be packed. Regardless of whether it was expensive or if you had to wait in line for hours, people would come every day to receive it. We can get this medicine, the mystic medicine of daimoku, in our own homes—and while sitting down, at that. All we need to pay for are candles and incense. So from the standpoint of cost, it is the least expensive method for happiness available. If someone just grumbles and fails to carry out the practice, it's a great waste." (LG, p. 87)

In Nichiren Daishonin's day, some carried out the practice of reading the Lotus Sutra in its entirety. The Daishonin indicates, however, that this is not necessary. He says that chanting the daimoku, or title of the sutra, once is the same as reading the entire sutra once and that chanting a thousand daimoku is the same as reading the sutra a thousand times. (LG, p. 85)

"If you ceaselessly chant daimoku, you will be continually reading the Lotus Sutra" (MW-I, 222). As indicated by the word *ceaselessly* in this passage from "The One Essential

Phrase," the important thing is to continue the practice of chanting daimoku throughout our lives. The amount of daimoku we chant each day will naturally vary somewhat over time. That's perfectly all right. The important thing is that we continue chanting daimoku throughout our lives. (LG, p. 85)

The air around us is filled with radio waves of various frequencies. While these are invisible, a television set can collect them and turn them into visible images. The practice of chanting daimoku to the Gohonzon aligns the rhythm of our own lives with the world of Buddhahood in the universe. It "tunes" our lives, so to speak, so that we can manifest the power of Buddhahood in our very beings. (LG, p. 80)

Everything becomes a source of value, everything is brought to life, when we base ourselves on daimoku. The Daishonin teaches that *myo* in Nam-myoho-renge-kyo means "to revive, to return to life." Nam-myoho-renge-kyo rejuvenates all knowledge; it revitalizes our daily lives. (LG, p. 80)

Doing gongyo and chanting daimoku to the Gohonzon represents the dawn, the start of a new day, in our lives. It is the sun rising. It is a profound sense of contentment in the depths of our beings that nothing can surpass. Even on these points alone we are truly fortunate. (6/23/96)

The Daishonin has taught us that through gongyo and chanting daimoku we can reach an elevated state in which, while engaged in our daily lives, we travel throughout the entire universe. When you worship the Gohonzon, the door to your microcosm is opened to the entire universe, the macrocosm, and you experience a great, boundless joy as if you were looking out over the entire cosmos. You feel great satisfaction and joy, a great wisdom, as if you held the entire universe in your palm. (2/20/90)

"Nam-myoho-renge-kyo is like the roar of a lion," the Daishonin says (MW-1, 119). It is by chanting powerful daimoku like a lion's roar that we can move the Buddhist deities, the protective forces of the universe. The voice is very important—it has profound power. While naturally being careful not to disturb your neighbors, I hope you will endeavor to chant cheerful and powerful daimoku that reaches all the Buddhist deities and Buddhas throughout the ten directions. (6/6/96)

The Daishonin states, "The voice does the Buddha's work" (*Gosho Zenshu,* p. 708). To chant the Mystic Law is to praise the Gohonzon. Hearing the sound of our daimoku, the heavenly deities will be set in motion and work to protect us. A weak and unclear voice will not move the heavenly deities. That is why it is important for us to chant daimoku with voices that are clear, strong and brimming with joy. (5/23/96)

When we practice gongyo and chant daimoku in front of the Gohonzon, the good and evil capacities of our lives begin to function as exalted forms of fundamental existence. Lives that are full of the pain of Hell, lives that are in the state of Hunger, lives warped by the state of Anger—such lives, too, begin to move in the direction of creating personal happiness and value. Lives being pulled toward misfortune and unhappiness are redirected and pulled in the opposite direction, toward good, when they make the Mystic Law their basis. (2/20/90)

How incredible it is to chant this wonderful daimoku each day! Nichiren Daishonin writes, "There is no greater happiness for human beings than chanting Nam-myoho-renge-kyo. The sutra [Lotus Sutra] says, 'The people there [in my land] are happy and at ease'" (MW-1, 161). There is no joy, happiness and ease surpassing what we attain through chanting daimoku. No matter how much you may pursue the things you love and skip gongyo to have a good time—all such fleeting, worldly pleasures pale beside the deep sense of satisfaction that comes from chanting daimoku. (5/26/98)

From one perspective, gongyo and daimoku are lyrics and songs. They are an ode to life. I hope, therefore, that your gongyo and daimoku will be such that even people who are not practicing will be favorably impressed by the sonorous and invigorating sound of your voices. That, too, will contribute to the spread of kosen-rufu. (3/8/98)

Gongyo and daimoku are a ceremony in which our lives commune with the universe. During gongyo, through our faith in the Gohonzon, we vigorously infuse the microcosm of our individual existence with the life force of the macrocosm, of the entire universe. If we do this regularly each morning and evening, our life force is strengthened. (DOY 2, ch. 19)

Even if you don't understand the literal meaning of what you say, your voices while doing gongyo and chanting daimoku to the Gohonzon reach all Buddhas, bodhisattvas and Buddhist deities throughout time and space and the protective functions within life and the universe. Then, though unseen, the entire universe will be activated in fulfilling your prayers. (DOY 2, ch. 19)

≈

The format of morning and evening gongyo of five prayers and three prayers, respectively, is not specified anywhere in Nichiren Daishonin's writings but is something that was developed gradually over later generations. If you genuinely don't have time to do a complete gongyo of five or three prayers, then a shortened gongyo is fine. Even just chanting some daimoku is quite okay, too. As long as we have faith in the Gohonzon, we are not going to suffer punishment or negative consequences on these accounts. So please put your mind at ease. Nichiren Daishonin says that even a single daimoku contains limitless benefits. (DOY 2, ch. 19)

≈

The Daishonin writes nothing in the Gosho about the specific amount we should chant. It is entirely up to each individual's awareness and sense of responsibility. Faith is a lifelong pursuit, so there's no need to be unnecessarily nervous or anxious about how much or how little daimoku you chant. (DOY 2, ch. 19)

≈

Exerting ourselves in the practice of gongyo each day amounts to what we might call a spiritual workout. It purifies and cleanses our lives, gets our motors running and puts us on the right course for the day. It gets our bodies and our minds working smoothly and puts us in rhythm, in sync, with the universe. (DOY 2, ch. 19)

≈

With daimoku you can turn all your worries and concerns into fuel to propel yourselves forward and you can transform them into life force, into greater depth of character and good fortune. (DOY 2, ch. 19)

~

It's best to keep your eyes open and to look at the Gohonzon. It's generally considered impolite not to look others in the eye when speaking to them. This is also true when we are facing and addressing the Gohonzon as we do gongyo or chant daimoku. If you do close your eyes occasionally, there's no need to worry. It's just that when we close our eyes, it can be more difficult to commune strongly with the Gohonzon. This, of course, does not apply to people who are blind or vision-impaired, who need to simply chant or do gongyo to the Gohonzon within their hearts. (DOY 2, ch. 20)

~

It's important to want to sit before the Gohonzon as though going to meet the original Buddha, Nichiren Daishonin, and that daimoku and gongyo be enjoyable. What's most important is that you continue in your Buddhist practice throughout life. There's no need to be overly concerned with formality. (DOY 2, ch. 20)

GOOD FRIENDS IN FAITH

The way of Buddhism is profound, and its wisdom is difficult to fathom. No matter how wise or knowledgeable one may appear, the wisdom of common mortals is trifling by comparison. Therefore, to pursue the way to Buddhahood, we have no choice but to make a "good friend" in faith. If we do so, the power of such a good friend will enable us to pursue the correct course toward enlightenment without error. (12/12/87)

A good friend in faith means someone who encourages your Buddhist practice and guides you toward the path of enlightenment. The same applies to our own practice of faith. The Gohonzon is always the basis of our practice. Needless to say, carrying out our correct faith is what is most important. However, if you no longer have someone who can teach you faith and guide your practice correctly, or if you follow the wrong person, it will become difficult for you to forge on along the great path of faith toward enlightenment. A good friend is, as it were, an important support in completing your faith and practice. Therefore, the most important point in faith is what kind of people you have as friends. In this sense, I hope you deeply understand that there is profound meaning behind the existence of the Soka Gakkai, which teaches correct faith and is advancing together along the path of kosen-rufu. (3/1/88)

Naturally, the Mystic Law is the foundation of all things. However, without "good friends" who can lead us to the Gohonzon, practically speaking, it would be impossible to attain Buddhahood. Fellow members who sincerely encourage us and the organization for kosen-rufu that enables us to follow the path of correct faith are the good friends we need. All fellow members who sincerely practice faith are good friends to one another. Though there may be differences in members' organizational positions and length of time practicing, we are all equal before the Gohonzon. There is absolutely no discrimination in the world of faith. Good friends are people who, in their respective capacities, encourage and pray for the development of one another. While traveling hand in hand along the path of eternal happiness, they invite others to join them so that they, too, may receive immeasurable benefit. Let us truly become such good friends to each other. (5/24/89)

The Nirvana Sutra states that even if we are killed by "evil elephants"—which in modern terms would correspond to automobiles, tanks, etc.—our bodies may be destroyed, but our minds will remain intact. However, if evil friends lead to our undoing, destroying both mind and body, we will fall into Hell. Therefore, we must above all fear falling under the influence of evil friends, and we should identify those who are crooked of heart and ward them off. Such persons appear as friends but function to destroy faith. Through the clever use of words, they try to persuade people to abandon their Buddhist practice. This is the nature of evil friends. Such bad friends are the greatest enemy of one's happiness and the greatest impediment to one's attaining Buddhahood. (6/18/91)

Good friends are those who instruct us in faith, strive with us to strengthen practice and study and work with us in harmony to advance kosen-rufu. The Soka Gakkai is the foremost gathering of good friends. (6/18/91)

Good friends base themselves on the law. Therefore, we base ourselves on the Gohonzon and on the Gosho. Evil friends are self-centered and egoistic. For these reasons, such people will speak and act differently, depending on the situation. As the Lotus Sutra and the Gosho make clear, it is only natural that the further kosen-rufu advances in any country, the more numerous will be the evil friends who appear. By seeing through the disguises of such individuals and defeating them, you will be able to open up a vast, cheerful, sunny green field of happiness for all members. (6/18/91)

Good friends in faith essentially are sincere, honest people without a trace of deceit who guide others toward the correct path, toward good. They are also people who lend their assistance or support to us so that we can practice the True Law with assurance. If you become close to a person who makes you feel "that person is always glowing and animated" or "when I'm with that person I feel strong and secure," then your faith will naturally deepen and you will develop bountiful wisdom. In carrying out this Buddhist practice, encountering good friends is the key to achieving Buddhahood. (7/28/91)

Evil companions or bad friends are the exact opposite of good friends. They lie, deceive people and destroy the good in others' hearts. They try their utmost to hamper or obstruct the correct practice of Buddhism by luring people toward evil and unhappiness. Many Gosho refer to the importance of continuing to seek out good friends and the importance of being able to astutely discern would-be evil companions and not be taken in by them. (7/28/91)

The Gohonzon functions to help us come to the awareness that we ourselves are the Buddha. Herein lies the true meaning of "the object of worship for observing one's mind." When we thus base ourselves on a correct understanding of the Gohonzon, we have no need whatsoever for priests who come along representing "external authority." What we need, rather, are good friends who help us gain self-awareness and live our lives with hope. (10/2/93)

Our lives are determined by the relationships we form. And the SGI is a cluster of relationships of the very best kind. In a society pervaded with cruel relationships, where many people delight in others' misfortunes, we find the greatest solidarity and peace of mind with our fellow members. We have to resolutely protect the noble gathering of SGI members. (8/21/96)

HOPE

We must live with vibrant hope. Nothing is stronger than hope. The Mystic Law is itself eternal hope. Happiness belongs to those who never despair no matter what happens. (5/26/97)

"Hope," Beethoven cried, "you forge the heart into steel." Hope is confidence. Hope is determination. Hope is courage. And faith is the ultimate expression of hope. Belief fortifies the heart. (2/24/96)

It all comes down to hope. If we SGI members advance with hope and buoyant spirits, then we have nothing to fear in the present or the future. The Law will continue to spread as long as those who uphold it remain vigorous and well. (1/6/96)

Faith is inextinguishable hope. The practice of faith is a struggle to realize our desires. The basis of this practice is prayer.

Through prayer, hope turns into confidence. This spirit of confidence unfolds in three thousand ways, finally resulting in the attainment of our hopes. Therefore, we must never give up. (LG, p. 91)

At the end of "The One Essential Phrase" Gosho the Dai-shonin says, "Do not doubt this in the least." We need great confidence and to live with great hope, whether we are young or old. When we manifest great hope, we can calmly survey our former sufferings. We can see that we have been taking small problems and blowing them up, worrying about them out of all proportion. (LG, p. 93)

There is no pessimism in Buddhism—not in the past, present or future. There is only optimism. Therefore, let us advance eternally with hope and optimism, come what may. (6/6/96)

Faith means infinite hope, and infinite hope resides in the SGI. As long as your faith is sincere, infinite glory, boundless good fortune and endless victory will unfold before you. You will never find yourselves at a dead end. (2/5/93)

I hope no matter what happens, you will always advance with hope. Especially I hope that the more desperate your cir-cumstances, the more you will press on with unflagging hope. Please keep challenging things with a bright and posi-tive spirit, always taking care at the same time to safeguard your health. (1/6/96)

We who embrace the Mystic Law will not suffer because of old age or death. As long as we keep our flame of faith alive, the fire of life force will burn brightly forever within us; we can live with great confidence that transcends birth and death. Faith is the engine that enables us to live with hope throughout our lives. (7/9/97)

If we seem to be weathering an endless winter, we mustn't abandon hope. As long as we have hope, spring will come without fail. (DOY 2, ch. 1)

HUMAN REVOLUTION

Those who at first may be completely overwhelmed by their environment or constantly defeated by their weaknesses but who then undergo dramatic personal transformation as a result of solid Buddhist practice can be wonderful inspirations for others. The most intense suffering, unbearable agony and seemingly insurmountable deadlock are actually brilliant opportunities for doing our human revolution. (DOY 2, ch. 21)

If you're the type whose resolve tends to melt away easily, if you find it difficult to stick to your goals, then just renew your determination each time you find yourself slipping. You will achieve your human revolution without fail if you keep struggling valiantly, pressing forward despite setbacks and disappointments, always thinking: "This time I'll make it! This time I will succeed!" (DOY 2, ch. 21)

Where can we find the royal road to reformation and change? Emerson declared: "Not he is great who can alter matter, but he who can alter my state of mind." He strongly urged us to undergo inner reformation. I want you to be assured that the challenge to which we set ourselves day after day—that of our human revolution—is the royal road to bringing about a reformation of our families, local regions and societies. An inner revolution is the most fundamental and at the same time the ultimate revolution for engendering change in all things. (2/5/93)

Only if you challenge your human revolution in a manner that is true to yourself will the people around you naturally begin to trust and respect you. That in itself is the surest way of laying the groundwork for the spread of Nichiren Daishonin's Buddhism. (2/26/90)

In Japan, the mountain potatoes known as taros are rough and dirty when harvested, but when they are placed in a basin of running water together and rolled against each other, the skin peels away, leaving the potatoes shining clean and ready for cooking. It's probably inappropriate to compare people to potatoes, but my point is that the only way for us to hone and polish our character is through our interactions with others. (DOY 2, ch. 19)

It doesn't matter in what area, just keep working on your personal revolution to transform and improve yourself in the way most natural for you. The important thing is that you change in some positive way. There is surely no more exhilarating life than one in which we write our own unique history of human revolution each day. The growth and transformation we achieve in this way can convince people

of the greatness of the Daishonin's Buddhism more eloquently than anything else. (12/16/96)

Unless we are strong, we cannot win in life, nor will we accomplish kosen-rufu. The essence of our human revolution is
to become as strong a human being as possible. President
Toda used to say, "Become individuals who are strong physically, intellectually and spiritually." (2/2/93)

A great human revolution in the life of one person can
change the destiny of humankind and our planet. It is Buddhism, the Lotus Sutra, that encourages and enables people to
become aware of their great power, to draw it forth and use
it. Buddhism gives people the means to develop themselves
thoroughly and opens their eyes to the limitless power inherent in their lives. (LG, p. 185)

In his "Precepts for Youth," President Toda cried out: "Stand
tall! Join the battle with me!" We must fight with love for the
people. Today, there are many youth who don't even love
their parents, so how can they love others? Our struggle is for
our human revolution—to surmount our lack of compassion
and develop in ourselves the mercy of the Buddha.
(LG, p. 147)

Through the concept of "the serene light of the moon of enlightenment," the Daishonin indicates a revolution of our
state of mind, a reformation in the depths of our lives. For
only through such an inner revolution may true happiness be
found. When we broadly expand our state of mind, hope and
vitality well up from within. Wisdom and compassion, joy

and good fortune surge forth from within our lives. (Dialogue 1, 1994)

~

Everything begins from the human revolution of one person. It is important first and foremost that each of you win in life and in society. I also hope each of you, with your brilliant presence, will illuminate all around you—the people you encounter, your local community, your country and all of humanity. (6/23/96)

~

President Makiguchi said there are three types of people in the world: those you want to have around, those whose presence or absence doesn't make a difference and those whose presence causes problems. Please become people others appreciate having around. This is the correct way of life for believers in Nichiren Daishonin's Buddhism, which teaches that Buddhahood is eternally inherent in our lives. (DOY 1, ch. 8)

~

President Toda said: "You don't have to worry about changing your personality. All you have to do is chant daimoku and live the best you can. Then, very naturally, you will see the negative aspects of your personality disappear, leaving you with the positive ones. You must have a clear purpose and work for the betterment of society." (DOY 1, ch. 10)

ICHINEN SANZEN

Those who say, "I'll do it," who are willing to take on a challenge even if alone are true winners. The determination, the commitment to take action yourself, is the force that leads to victory. As Buddhism teaches in the principle of 3,000 realms in a single moment of life (*ichinen sanzen*), our mind or attitude can change everything. (1/8/98)

The Gohonzon is a clear mirror. It reveals perfectly our state of faith and projects this out into the universe. This demonstrates the principle of 3,000 realms in a single moment of life. (2/27/90)

Buddhism teaches that life at each moment embraces all phenomena. This is the doctrine of 3,000 realms in a single moment of life, which is the Lotus Sutra's ultimate teaching and Buddhism's essence. Because of the profound way our lives interact with people around us, it is vital that we reach out to others, that we engage our environments and our local communities. A self-absorbed practice or theory without action is definitely not Buddhism. (1/17/98)

"What kind of future do I envision?" we may ask ourselves. "What kind of self am I trying to develop? What do I want to accomplish in my life?" We should paint this vision of our lives on the canvas of our hearts as specifically as possible. This "painting" becomes the design for our future. The power of the heart enables us to actually create a wonderful masterpiece following that design. This is the doctrine of 3,000 realms in a single moment of life. (LG, p. 129)

Fundamentally speaking, infinite variety derives from the one Law and the true entity of life, as described by the one hundred worlds and 1,000 factors as well as *ichinen sanzen*. This is the same in all societies. Viewed from this perspective, it is important that we respect anyone who is struggling on the forefront of our movement for kosen-rufu. This attitude of respect will become a great driving force behind the spread of the Mystic Law. (2/13/90)

KARMA

The nature of human beings is truly bewildering and complex. Those things we seem to have no control over are called karma. The conclusion we reach is that, when we live in accordance with the great inscrutable Law of Nam-myoho-renge-kyo, we can harmonize everything and change the poison of any bad karma into medicine. (8/7/92)

It takes a great deal of time and effort to overcome sufferings of a karmic nature, whose roots lie deep in causes we made in the past. There is a big difference between, for example, the time it takes for a scratch to heal and the time required to recover from a serious disease. The same applies to changing our karma through faith and practice. (DOY 2, ch. 20)

Each person's level of faith and individual karma differs. By chanting daimoku, however, we can bring forth from within a powerful sense of hope and move our lives in a positive, beneficial direction. (DOY 2, ch. 20)

LIFE-CONDITION

What is the purpose of life? It is happiness. What is it that determines whether one is happy? It is one's state of life. Even though they might dwell in the same environment, people feel differing degrees of happiness or unhappiness depending on their state of life. The practice of faith is a continuous effort for self-development that enables one to limitlessly broaden and expand one's state of life. (6/13/91)

Life flashes by in an instant. By devoting our lives to Buddhism, we will live a life of complete fulfillment. We are selling ourselves short if we fail to attain this wonderful state of life. (5/16/96)

Spirit means inner state of life, or one's heart. It decides what we devote our lives to. It is the fundamental prayer on which we base our existence. A person's spirit is invisible but becomes manifest at a crucial moment. Not only that, it also controls everything about a person, each moment of every day—it is the fundamental determinant of one's life. (LG, p. 129)

We need to cultivate a state of life where we can thoroughly enjoy ourselves at all times. We should have such joy that even at the time of death we can declare with a happy smile: "That was wonderful! Where shall I go next?" This is the state of mind of a person with strong faith. Such individuals will be reborn without delay and in a form and in a place exactly according with their desires. Faith enables us to attain the kind of generous and all-embracing state of mind where we enjoy everything in our lives. (5/26/97)

Much human misery arises from people despairing over things that despair cannot help. We should not worry about things that no amount of worrying will resolve. The important thing is to build a golden palace of joy in our hearts that nothing can disturb—a state of life like a clear blue sky above the storm, an oasis in the desert, a fortress looking down on high waves. (LG, p. 243)

~

What is true joy in life? This is a difficult question—and one which has occupied a great many thinkers and philosophers. Joy can quickly give way to suffering. Joy is short but suffering is long. What passes for joy in society is superficial. It cannot compare with the joy derived from the Mystic Law. The key then lies in cultivating a state of mind where we can declare without reservation that life itself is a joy. This is the purpose of our Buddhist practice. (7/9/97)

~

When we change our state of life, our view of everything alters. Seen with the eyes of common mortals, a common mortal appears simply as a common mortal; but seen with the eyes of the Buddha, ordinary people, just as they are, are Buddhas. (LG, p. 44)

~

We are all human beings; in that regard, we are all the same. The only real difference lies in people's life-conditions. Our life-condition continues beyond death, into eternity. Therefore, as the Daishonin says, "Faith alone is what really matters." (9/26/96)

~

It is important that we live cheerfully. With a strong spirit of optimism, we need to continually direct our minds in a bright, positive, beneficial direction and help those around us to do so, too. We should strive to develop a state of life where we feel a sense of joy no matter what happens. (9/15/97)

~

It is important to have a sufficiently elevated life-condition so that you will be able to calmly accept whatever happens in life, striving to put problems into their proper perspective and solving them with a positive attitude. Happiness blossoms forth from such a strong and all-encompassing life-condition. (2/12/90)

The most important thing is to develop our state of life. When human beings think of nothing but themselves, they increasingly become entrenched in small-mindedness and their small, lesser selves. (3/9/93)

Those who work toward a great and all-encompassing objective — for the sake of the Law, for others, for society—can forge generous hearts and great, magnanimous selves through the mystic function of their minds. Those with big hearts are assured of savoring great happiness. (3/9/93)

By developing one's life-condition, sufferings that may have once been a heavy burden when you had a lesser state of mind will appear minor, and you will be able to calmly rise above them. I hope all of you will lead lives in which you show splendid proof of this mystic function of the mind. (3/9/93)

MIND OF FAITH

There may be times when you feel reluctant to do gongyo or take part in activities for kosen-rufu. That state of mind is reflected in the entire universe, as if on the surface of a clear mirror. The heavenly deities will then also feel reluctant to play their part, and they will naturally fail to exert their full powers of protection. (2/27/90)

No matter how healthy, intelligent or affluent we may be, if our minds are weak, then our happiness will also be frail and brittle. Our minds of faith, moreover, enable us to bring out the full positive potential in all things and situations, so it is crucial that we strive to forge our minds of faith. (2/2/93)

Mahatma Gandhi (1869–1948) once said that people become the people they expect themselves to be. Your mind, your *ichinen*, determines your future, your life. (3/9/93)

Faith is the secret to happiness for all people. When you truly forge your mind of faith, you will become an eternal victor throughout the three existences of past, present and future. Strong faith enables you to display appropriate wisdom, so that you can take advantage of change and move forward in the direction of hope and victory. (1/31/93)

It may seem perfectly all right to put ourselves and our wishes first, to simply follow the dictates of our emotions and cravings, but the truth is that there is nothing more unreliable than our own minds. Life doesn't always go like clockwork and things will not necessarily turn out as we had hoped or planned. Consequently, Nichiren Daishonin frequently stressed that you should become the master of your mind, not let your mind master you. We mustn't allow ourselves to be ruled by a self-centered mind. Rather, we have to discipline our mind and gain mastery over it. This is the Daishonin's strict admonition. (8/27/97)

As long as our mind of faith is connected to the Gohonzon, our benefits will never disappear. That's why it is vital to persevere in our Buddhist practice throughout our lives, no matter what, even if on some days our physical condition or other circumstances prevent us from doing gongyo and chanting daimoku to our full satisfaction. Those who continue to challenge themselves to the end savor ultimate victory. (1/31/93)

The mind of faith is invisible. Those who advance together with this organization dedicated to kosen-rufu will evolve the correct mind of faith that matches the time. With this mind of faith, you can fill the canvas of your lives with portraits of happiness in which all your wishes are fulfilled. (1/31/93)

MISSION

The mission of leaders is to show actual proof of victory for the sake of the members. They must never make the members feel disappointed. (1/19/95)

A life lived without purpose or value, the kind in which one doesn't know the reason why one was born, is joyless and lackluster. To just live, eat and die without any real sense of purpose surely represents a life pervaded by the world of Animality. On the other hand, to do, create or contribute something that benefits others, society and ourselves and to dedicate ourselves as long as we live to that challenge—that is a life of true satisfaction, a life of value. It is a humanistic and lofty way to live. (6/15/96)

Those who wake up each morning with work to accomplish and a mission to fulfill are the happiest of all. SGI members are like this. For us, each day is one of supreme purpose and satisfaction. For those who abandon faith, each day is hollow, dreary and lonely. Jealous of our happiness, they begin to attack the SGI. For us, each day is *kuon ganjo*—time without beginning; each day is the New Year. Please exert yourselves vigorously with the determination to live each day to the fullest, so that you may compose a golden diary of life. (1/6/96)

First, you must be strong. There is no hope of winning in this chaotic world if you are weak. No matter what others do or say, it is important to develop your ability and put that ability to use. Strong faith, of course, is the best means for drawing out one's inner strength. You each have a very important mission, and I hope you will awaken to it and take pride in that mission. (2/17/96)

The greater our efforts to advance kosen-rufu, the greater the benefit and eternal good fortune we accumulate in our lives. The more outstanding people we foster, the stronger and healthier we become. The more aware we are of our responsibility, the more joy we experience. Such are the workings of the Buddhist Law. (3/20/96)

There may be times when life seems gloomy and dull. When we feel stuck in some situation or another, when we are negative toward everything, when we feel lost and bewildered, not sure which way to turn. At such times we must transform our passive mind-sets and determine, "I will proceed along this path," "I will pursue my mission today." When we do so, a genuine springtime arrives in our hearts and flowers start to blossom. (6/28/95)

Buddhism teaches the principle of cherry, plum, peach and damson, that all things have a unique beauty and mission. Every person has a singular mission, his or her individuality and way of life. That is the natural order of things. (DOY 2, ch.1)

OBSTACLES

In the "Record of the Orally Transmitted Teachings," the Daishonin says, "One should regard meeting obstacles as true peace and comfort" (*Gosho Zenshu*, p. 750). You may wonder how encountering obstacles could be a source of peace and comfort. But the truth of the matter is that by struggling against and overcoming difficulties we transform our destiny and attain Buddhahood. Confronting adversity, therefore, ultimately represents peace and comfort. (1/27/96)

Life has the capacity, like flames reaching toward heaven, to transform suffering and pain into the energy needed for value-creation, into light that illuminates darkness. Like wind traversing vast spaces unhindered, life has the power to uproot and overturn all obstacles and difficulties. Like clear flowing water, it can wash away all stains and impurities. And finally, life, like the great earth that sustains all vegetation, impartially protects all people with its compassionate, nurturing force. (2/11/98)

~

Many things happen in life. There are joyous days and times of suffering. Sometimes unpleasant things occur. But that's what makes life so interesting. The dramas we encounter are part and parcel of being human. If we experienced no change or drama in our lives, if nothing unexpected ever happened, we would be like automatons, our lives would be unbearably monotonous and dull. Therefore, please develop a strong self so that you can enact the drama of your life with confidence and poise in the face of all life's vicissitudes. (3/24/97)

~

The famous poet Shelley said, "If Winter comes, can Spring be far behind?" No matter how long and bitter winter may be, spring always follows. This is the law of the universe, the joyful law of life. (DOY 2, ch. 1)

~

What makes someone a hero? Napoleon maintained, "True heroism consists in being superior to the misfortunes of life." To have never tasted failure, defeat or misfortune is not heroism or happiness, for that matter. A truly heroic way of life lies in squarely confronting and courageously overcoming the pounding vicissitudes that life always throws in our paths. (2/24/96)

~

Buddhism is, in a sense, an eternal struggle between the Buddha and demons; in other words, a contest between positive and negative forces. If we fail to be assailed by negative influences, we cannot be said to be truly practicing Nichiren Daishonin's Buddhism. No purpose is served by constantly vacillating between feelings of sadness and joy, allowing ourselves to become victims of changing circumstances. Buddhist practice lies in bravely facing and overcoming adversity. (3/18/96)

Encountering great obstacles for the sake of Buddhism in this life guarantees that we will achieve enlightenment. Coming up against the three powerful enemies makes this true for all eternity; their very appearance serves as clear proof of this fact. (3/3/96)

In any earnest struggle, there come crucial challenges—mountains that must be scaled and conquered if we are to win. In Buddhist practice, too, we face such crucial challenges—namely the struggle against the three powerful enemies. If we hope to advance kosen-rufu and attain Buddhahood, then we must scale this mountain. (1/27/96)

Attaining "peace and security in this life" doesn't mean having a life free from difficulties but means that whatever difficulties arise, without being shaken in the least, you can summon up the unflinching courage and conviction to fight against and overcome them. This is the state of life of "peace and security in this life." (LG, p. 241)

Faith makes people strong. And people of genuine faith shine the most when they encounter great difficulties. Certainly, it is better not to have obstacles. But from another standpoint, difficulties are benefits. By challenging and overcoming them, we can forge a character pure and immutable as gold. (LG, p. 127)

~

Daimoku is like fire. When you burn the firewood of earthly desires, then the fire of happiness—that is, of enlightenment—burns brightly. Sufferings thus become the raw material for constructing happiness. For someone who does not have faith in the Mystic Law, sufferings may be only sufferings. But for a person with strong faith, sufferings function to enable him or her to become happier still. (LG, p. 91)

~

Even places that have been shrouded in darkness for billions of years can be illuminated. Even a stone from the bottom of a river can be used to produce fire. Our present sufferings, no matter how dark, have certainly not continued for billions of years—nor will they linger forever. The sun will definitely rise. In fact, its ascent has already begun. (LG, p. 91)

~

How do we tackle our problems? This challenge makes for a rich life. Buddhism teaches that "earthly desires are enlightenment." The greater our sufferings, the greater the happiness we transform them into—through the power of the daimoku. (3/9/93)

~

Eiji Yoshikawa (1892–1962), the renowned Japanese author of many epic historic novels, asserted, "Great character is forged through hardships." Surviving a life of hardships and difficulties, of stormy ups and downs, is what produces a person of great depth and character. True happiness is also found in such an unshakable state of life. (3/17/96)

~

We are people of faith, and faith is the ultimate conviction. Nothing could be sadder or more shortsighted, therefore, than complaining or giving up when we encounter some small obstacle in our path. A genuine Buddhist is a person of wisdom and conviction. (12/16/96)

Freedom doesn't mean an absence of all restrictions. It means possessing unshakable conviction in the face of any obstacle. This is true freedom. (7/19/96)

Please remember that patience is, in and of itself, a great challenge and it often holds the key to breaking through a seeming impasse. (3/21/96)

PERSEVERANCE

Our Buddhist practice takes place in the midst of our busy daily lives. It is all too easy for us to grow lazy and neglect it. Therefore, there is perhaps no more difficult practice when it comes to continuing. If we challenge ourselves to keep practicing even a little each day, before we realize it we have built a path to happiness in the depths of our lives; we have established a solid embankment that will prevent our ever being swept away toward unhappiness. (DOY 2, ch. 20)

There is no need to seek impatiently for greatness, fame or wealth. The earth and sun do not hurry; they follow their own path at their own pace. If the earth were to accelerate and complete one rotation in three hours instead of twenty-four, we would be in big trouble! The most important thing in life, too, is to find a sure and certain path and confidently advance along it. (3/17/96)

~

It is important to take a long-range view. No great achievement is accomplished overnight or without difficulty. Should benefit be obtained easily, without our making serious efforts in our Buddhist practice, we'd probably easily abandon our faith and end up miserable. (6/15/96)

~

President Toda was always a friend and ally of those who were suffering or in pain. He warmly embraced each person. Once he offered the following words of encouragement to a member: "Don't be impatient. Since you have embraced the Gohonzon, your situation will definitely improve. There's no need to worry. Sure, there will be hard times, times when you feel like crying. But as long as you have the Gohonzon, your life will become bright and joyful." (1/30/93)

~

Because life is long, you should not be impatient. What matters most is that you embrace the Gohonzon throughout your life. It is vitally important to continually challenge yourself to chant even a little more daimoku and to pray before the Gohonzon for the fulfillment of your desires. (2/25/90)

~

It's foolish to be obsessed with past failures. And it's just as foolish to be self-satisfied with one's small achievements. Buddhism teaches that the present and the future are important, not the past. It teaches us a spirit of unceasing challenge to win over the present and advance ever toward the future.

Those who neglect this spirit of continual striving steer their lives in a ruinous direction. (2/17/96)

It is important to become strong and to not be defeated. Don't become the kind of people who are always depending or leaning on others or who weakly and timidly leave hard work and responsibility to others. Whatever obstacles you may encounter, please use them as a launching pad for your growth and keep advancing, bravely enduring all hardships, telling yourselves, "I'll show them what I'm made of!" (DOY 1, ch. 2)

There is no reason to be impatient or in a hurry. As long as one wins in the end, that's what matters. Those who do so are true victors. (6/15/96)

Buddhism stresses the importance of the present and the future. There is little point in dwelling on the past. Far more constructive is looking to the future and moving forward. What is vital is that we achieve a bright and glorious future through our efforts and perseverance today. (6/15/96)

No matter what the circumstances, you should never concede defeat. Never conclude that you've reached a dead end, that everything is finished. You possess a glorious future. Precisely because of that, you must persevere and study. Life is eternal. We need to focus on the two existences of the present and the future and not get caught up in worry about the past. We must always have the spirit to begin anew "from this moment," to initiate a new struggle each day. (4/2/95)

We must put down firm roots; we must be strong. Inner strength is a prerequisite for happiness, a prerequisite for upholding justice and one's beliefs. One of the Buddha's titles is "He Who Can Forbear." To courageously endure, persevere and overcome all difficulties—the Buddha is the ultimate embodiment of the virtue of forbearance. The power of faith gives us the strength to weather and survive any storm. Perseverance is the essence of a Buddha. (2/2/93)

Life isn't always smooth. If it were, we would never grow and develop as human beings. If we succeed we are envied; if we fail we are ridiculed and attacked. Sadly, this is how people are. Unexpected grief and suffering may lie ahead of you. But it is precisely then, when you encounter such trying times, that you must not be defeated. Never give up. Never retreat. (3/17/96)

In all things patience is the key to victory. Those who cannot endure cannot hope to win. Ultimate triumph belongs to those who can forbear. (3/8/98)

There is no need for you to be impatient. If you achieve something very easily, right from the start, you will find no sense of fulfillment or joy. It is in making tenacious, all-out efforts for construction that profound happiness lies. (2/15/90)

Doing gongyo every day is a challenge. Introducing others to the practice is a challenge. Getting people to subscribe to organ publications is a challenge. Attending meetings is a challenge. Sometimes it can all become too much, leaving one feeling negative and wanting to take a break! Since we are human beings, it's only natural that we might feel this way on occasion. The important thing, however, is not to spin out of the orbit of faith. I hope you will continue to pursue the path of Buddhahood steadily and patiently, encouraging one another on your journey. (6/15/96)

What was the secret to Edison's success? He explained that it was that he never gave up before he succeeded in what he was trying to do. Not giving up—that's the only way. Once you give up you are defeated. This is equally true in the realm of faith. Quitting is not faith. We have to keep chanting until our prayers are answered. That is the correct way of prayer. (2/3/98)

What was

Faith is perseverance. The key to victory in any struggle in life is persistence. That is why Nichiren Daishonin stresses the importance of having faith that flows ceaselessly like water rather than faith that flares up briefly like fire. To advance continuously it is important never to become exhausted. Carrying out activities until late at night does not equal strong faith. (4/13/96)

Gongyo is important, but essentially the most vital thing is to continue to embrace the Gohonzon your whole life long and never, ever abandon it. It is totally self-defeating if you practice passionately with faith like fire for a time and end up discarding your faith later on. (DOY 2, ch. 19)

PRACTICE

As the Daishonin teaches through the principle of practicing for oneself and others, our Buddhist practice exists not only so we can bring forth the state of Buddhahood in our lives but to help others to do the same. This is the purpose of spreading the Daishonin's teachings and giving guidance and encouragement. (Dialogue 1, 1994)

Because it isn't easy to get into a highly ranked school, students study with all their might, gaining as a result of their efforts an abundance of knowledge and ability. Faith follows basically the same formula: Practice is essential to attaining Buddhahood. (6/15/96)

Our lives grow to the degree that we give hope and courage to others and enable them to develop their lives. Therefore, while we speak of practicing for others, it is we ourselves who ultimately benefit. With this understanding comes the ability to take action with a sense of appreciation. (Dialogue 1, 1994)

Buddhism teaches that we should live our lives with the perfect serenity and composure of the Himalayas, not bending in the least before the eight winds, which can function to extinguish the flame of our Buddhist practice. (3/3/96)

We live in an age in which people can no longer clearly distinguish between right or wrong, good or evil. This is a global trend. If things continue in this way, humanity is destined for chaos and moral decay. In the midst of such an age, you are upholding and earnestly practicing Nichiren Daishonin's Buddhism, a teaching of the highest good. (6/26/96)

As far as the fundamental teachings of Buddhism and the Gosho are concerned, I hope that, regarding them as absolutely correct, you will first and foremost strive to put them into practice. I urge you to do so, because this is the shortest route to understanding the essence of Buddhism in the depths of your life. (2/15/90)

Nothing can match the strength of those whose lives have been shaped and forged through challenging and overcoming hardships. Such people fear nothing. The purpose of our Buddhist practice is to develop such strength and fortitude. To cultivate such an invincible core is in itself a victory. It is also the greatest benefit. Those who succeed in this endeavor will savor unsurpassed happiness; they manifest the supreme state of Buddhahood. (8/29/96)

Practicing Buddhism means being victorious. In advancing one step at a time amid the realities of our daily lives, in showing concrete actual proof, in becoming victors and successes we are demonstrating with our very beings the validity of Nichiren Daishonin's Buddhism and serving as a source of hope and inspiration for those who follow us on the path of faith. (7/3/96)

Buddhism means putting the teachings into practice. Practice equals faith. With sincere prayer and action, our desires cannot possibly fail to be fulfilled. (1/27/93)

PRAYER

Prayers based on the Mystic Law are not abstract. They are a concrete reality in our lives. To offer prayers is to conduct a dialogue, an exchange, with the universe. When we pray, we embrace the universe with our lives and our determinations. Prayer is a struggle to expand our lives. (LG, p. 92)

It is important that we offer prayers with great confidence. The powers of the Buddha and the Law are activated in direct proportion to the strength of our faith and practice. Strong faith is like high voltage—it turns on a brilliant light in our lives. (LG, p. 88)

Prayers are invisible, but if we pray steadfastly they will definitely effect clear results in our lives and surroundings over time. This is the principle of the true entity of all phenomena. Faith means having confidence in this invisible realm. Those who impatiently pursue only visible gains, who put on airs or who are caught up in vanity and formalism, will definitely become deadlocked. (LG, p. 88)

When we chant daimoku with appreciation at having the rare opportunity to dedicate our lives to the noble mission of wholeheartedly devoting ourselves to others' happiness, immense vitality wells forth. From the depths of our lives, we tap the wisdom to encourage others and show actual proof. (LG, p. 78)

Nichiren Daishonin writes: "Kyo'o Gozen's misfortunes will change into fortune. Muster your faith and pray to this

Gohonzon. Then what is there that cannot be achieved?"
(MW-1, 120). The first thing is to pray. From the moment
we begin to pray, things start moving. The darker the night,
the closer the dawn. From the moment we chant daimoku
with a deep and powerful resolve, the sun begins to rise in
our hearts. (6/15/96)

Prayer is the sun of hope. To chant daimoku each time we
face a problem, overcoming it and elevating our life-condition as a result—this is the path of "changing earthly desires
into enlightenment" taught in Nichiren Daishonin's Buddhism. (6/15/96)

We practice this Buddhism to make our prayers and dreams
come true and to achieve the greatest possible happiness. The
purpose of Nichiren Daishonin's Buddhism is to enable us to
realize victory in life. The fact that our prayers are answered
is proof of the correctness of this teaching. (6/12/96)

As long as we pray earnestly and sincerely with our entire being, if we have strong and genuine faith, even though results
may not be immediately visible, they will definitely manifest
without fail throughout generations of our children and our
children's children. I would like all of you to have absolute
confidence in this. (5/23/96)

There are many elements involved in a prayer being answered, but the important thing is to keep praying until it is.
By continuing to pray, you can reflect on yourself with unflinching honesty and begin to move your life in a positive
direction on the path of earnest, steady effort. Even if your

prayer doesn't produce concrete results immediately, your continual prayer will at some time manifest itself in a form greater than you had ever hoped. (6/16/98)

Why is it that sometimes our prayers seem to be unanswered? This is a manifestation of the Buddha's wisdom—so that we can deepen our prayers, become stronger people, live more profound lives and secure deeper, more lasting good fortune. If our slightest prayer were answered immediately, we'd become lazy and degenerate. And we couldn't hope to build a life of great dignity and substance. (6/16/98)

Prayer is not of the realm of logic or intellect. It transcends these. Prayer is an act in which we give expression to the pressing and powerful wishes in the depths of our being and yearn for their fulfillment. (DOY 2, ch. 19)

When looking at the Gohonzon, directing your gaze wherever is most natural for you is fine. You can look at the characters of Nam-myoho-renge-kyo in the center, or you can gaze at the entire Gohonzon. As long as we chant with strong faith, our prayers are fully communicated. (DOY 2, ch. 20)

Being human, it's natural for our minds to wander, for all sorts of thoughts and memories to surface during prayer. You can share all those thoughts with the Gohonzon. There is no set form or pattern for how we should pray. Buddhism emphasizes being natural. Therefore, simply chant earnestly without pretense, just as you are. In time, as your faith develops, you'll find it easier to focus your mind when you chant. (DOY 2, ch. 20)

It's natural for prayers to center on your own desires and dreams. There's no need to pretend that you're praying for something lofty when you're not. You're only fooling yourself if you pretend. By chanting naturally, without affectation or reservation, for what you seek most of all, you'll gradually come to develop a higher, more expansive life-condition. (DOY 2, ch. 20)

It's fine to chant with the resolve to become bigger-hearted or for the welfare of your friends and for kosen-rufu and the happiness and prosperity of all humankind. You are free to chant for whatever you wish. It's all up to you. Doing gongyo and chanting daimoku are not obligations. They are your wonderful right. (DOY 2, ch. 20)

In Nichiren Daishonin's Buddhism, it is said that no prayer goes unanswered. But this is very different from having every wish instantly gratified as if by magic. If you chant to win the lottery tomorrow, or to score 100 percent on a test tomorrow without having studied, the odds are small that it will happen. Nonetheless, viewed from a deeper, longer-term perspective, all your prayers serve to propel you in the direction of happiness. (DOY 2, ch. 20)

Sometimes our immediate prayers are realized and sometimes they aren't. When we look back later, however, we can say with absolute conviction that everything turned out for the best. (DOY 2, ch. 20)

Buddhism is reason. Our faith is reflected in our daily lives, in our actual circumstances. Our prayers cannot be answered if we fail to make efforts appropriate to our situation. (DOY 2, ch. 20)

PROPAGATION

The dual nature of our practice, for ourselves and for others, will never change. Practice for ourselves constitutes chanting daimoku and doing gongyo with faith in the Gohonzon, while practice for others constitutes teaching others about the Mystic Law. (DOY 2, ch. 20)

How can one propagate the Daishonin's Buddhism without knowing about other teachings in the world? When based on the Mystic Law, all laws of the world and society begin to function in their most valuable way. All endeavors in human society—in the fields of politics, economics, learning and so on—become revitalized. They come to display their full potential and attain new life. The lifeblood of Buddhism pulses within society. Cut off from secular affairs, Buddhism cannot reveal its full validity. (10/1/91)

People may sincerely believe they are practicing Buddhism, but if they do not tell others about Buddhism, neglect to take action for kosen-rufu and give no encouragement to fellow members, then they cannot be said to be correctly practicing the Daishonin's Buddhism. Attending discussion meetings, giving individual guidance and sharing thoughts and opinions with our friends—these and other activities we of the SGI undertake are in direct accordance with the Daishonin's teachings. And the Daishonin would surely applaud our efforts. (3/10/92)

Nichiren Daishonin said to one of his lay followers: "I entrust you with the propagation of Buddhism in your province. Because the seeds of Buddhahood sprout in response to the proper influence, one expounds the teaching of the one vehicle" (MW-5, 151). Forming connections with other human beings is important. For each of us, everything starts with developing connections with others, forging bonds of friendship and winning their trust. (6/15/96)

When something needs saying, it is our duty to speak out. When something is right, we should say so; and when something is wrong or mistaken, we should likewise point that out. Cheating, lies or scheming should be denounced with alacrity. It is precisely because we have done this that the Soka Gakkai and SGI have developed to the extent that they have. To say what must be said—that is the spirit of propagation and the essence of the Soka Gakkai and SGI. (9/25/97)

It is our hearts that change others' hearts. Friendship changes people. Travelers who pull their capes over their shoulders and brace themselves determinedly against the cold wind naturally relax and change their outlook and actions when warmed by the sun. (2/5/93)

We exert ourselves to spread Nichiren Daishonin's Buddhism and carry out other activities so that we can accumulate good fortune and become happy. We do all this for our own sake, not for the sake of the organization and most certainly not for the sake of our leaders. (2/25/90)

Propagation is a practice that we carry out on the instruction of Nichiren Daishonin. Whether people to whom you explain Nichiren Daishonin's Buddhism decide to take faith depends mainly upon their life tendency and their capacity to understand and believe in Buddhism. In any case, whether or not a person determines to take faith in Buddhism after listening to an explanation, the benefit that the person sharing Buddhism receives is the same. (2/25/90)

Propagation is the action of the Buddha's envoys. We should treasure and most highly respect those who carry out this noble, benevolent practice. (2/25/90)

"You've done well. You were able to plant the seed of Buddhahood in your friend's heart. That's a splendid thing." So saying, you should praise and encourage one another, sharing one another's joy as brothers and sisters. Touched by such a family-like atmosphere, more and more people will begin to take faith in true Buddhism. Love and peace are the lifeblood of a true home. (2/25/90)

There is no need whatsoever to be impatient in propagating Nichiren Daishonin's Buddhism. Rather, it is preferable that strict standards be applied when granting admission to the organization, to the extent that those eager to join will find that their wish is not easily granted. One must absolutely never have an easygoing or careless attitude when it comes to allowing people to receive the Gohonzon. (2/26/90)

Propagation is an act to be conducted with the utmost respect for other people, out of sincere reverence for the Buddha nature inherent in their lives. Therefore, we should strictly observe courtesy and good common sense in propagation activities. (2/27/90)

In propagating the Mystic Law, understanding that we are addressing that person's Buddha nature, we should politely and calmly carry out dialogue—sometimes mercifully correcting that person with fatherly strictness. In the course of such human interaction, the Buddha nature in that person, reflecting our own sincerity, will bow to us in return. (2/27/90)

Toward Hei no Saemon and wicked priests, the Daishonin was a most severe foe. Yet he teaches his followers that in spreading the teaching to others, they should conduct themselves courteously. For example, he advised one person to always speak "mildly but firmly in a quiet voice with a calm gaze and an even expression" (MW-4, 122). (LG, p. 53)

Whether or not someone succeeds in helping others take faith in the teachings of Buddhism, the simple fact that he or she practices is in itself most praiseworthy. If you can feel heartfelt joy in being able to expound the Law and share it with others, your blessings will increase still further. Joyfully engaging in propagation and other activities is the spirit of Buddhism. (2/13/90)

PROTECTION

The protection of the four bodhisattvas, especially that of Bodhisattva Jogyo, essentially means that the original Buddha, Nichiren Daishonin, will definitely protect us. It is none other than our strong faith that elicits this protection. For instance, should we fall ill or encounter some other kind of problem, the four bodhisattvas—in other words, the Daishonin—will fight alongside us to overcome them. We are not alone and without friends. We can confidently overcome difficulties and turn everything to gain momentum toward happiness. When we have firm conviction in this, we will experience a sense of boundless courage; we will remain unafraid of anything. (6/2/92)

Impressed by our earnest prayers, all Buddhas, bodhisattvas and heavenly deities throughout the three existences and the ten directions will praise us and press their palms together in reverence. Moved by our endeavors for kosen-rufu, all Buddhas, bodhisattvas and heavenly deities will rejoice and be inspired to assist and protect us. (2/5/96)

Let us continue to chant with joy for being SGI members. Such joyous faith will cause the heavenly deities and Buddhas and bodhisattvas throughout the ten directions and the three existences of past, present and future to protect us through both life and death. They will ever embrace us. Those who possess such faith will shine as Buddhas for all eternity. Above all else, we must remember that the Daishonin is aware of all of our sincere efforts for kosen-rufu. (2/5/96)

SEEKING SPIRIT

Telling oneself, "This is as far as I need to go; I don't have to go any further," indicates overconfidence and leads to arrogance. A life filled with the ceaseless seeking spirit to improve oneself, to challenge oneself, to study harder, to search—such an existence is indeed worthy of respect from the standpoint of Buddhism. This attitude is the driving force for living a creative life. (6/7/92)

The most fundamental thing is to have a sense of humility toward the Law and toward truth. It is to our own benefit to advance along the path of faith with sincere humility and a boundless seeking mind. The greater our seeking spirit, the greater fortune we gain and the stronger and happier we become. (2/16/92)

A person of seeking spirit—one who strives to thoroughly pursue some end or to master some discipline—is a person of victory. On the other hand, a person of arrogance inevitably becomes deadlocked. (7/17/92)

I also hope that you will have the willingness and open-mindedness to learn from everyone, to take lessons from others. You might admire a fellow member's sincere attitude toward faith or the happy and harmonious family someone else has. You can learn something from everyone, even if it is merely a person's good posture or the care and attention they pay to their make-up or grooming. To have the humility to learn something from anyone is a measure of how big a person is. (9/18/93)

Just because people are scholars, are famous or have wealth or power doesn't mean that they can fully perceive the law of cause and effect within their lives. Human beings can be quite arrogant, but if they don't sincerely and humbly seek this fundamental, vital Law, then they are being foolish. This is regrettable, because this grave error can cause a fatal deviation from the correct path of life. (4/29/88)

Some might think: "I have been practicing longer than others" or "My position is higher than others." Such thoughts indicate that they have already lost their fresh seeking mind. One's mind is unfathomable; it is also quite changeable. If you lose your seeking spirit, no matter how much you have been striving, no matter how many merits you have won in faith, your faith will retreat rapidly until you cannot understand what faith is all about. (6/21/88)

Just because you have faith doesn't mean you can rest easy and spend your entire life proceeding along the Great Way to Buddhahood. If you have faith in name alone, that has no true merit. Worse yet, in most cases you will face that most important event, your own death, in great suffering. Such faith is of no use at all. Once you have been blessed with encountering the True Law, you should devote the rest of your life, without regret, to seeking the Way. Be filled with the joy of faith and bravely spread the Law. That is our duty in accepting the True Law. (5/23/90)

To seek the Daishonin, to live alongside the Daishonin in accordance with his teachings—such faith itself becomes the wings of happiness that lead us to the world of Buddhahood. It can even be said that such strong faith is itself the manifestation of Buddhahood. Such a person will most assuredly enjoy great happiness. (8/24/90)

Whether humility is a virtue or arrogance is an evil must be judged in terms of the circumstances under which they appear. When we confront evil, we need a forcefulness that may verge on arrogance to point out, attack and correct the injustices evil breeds, just as the Gosho instructs. This is the stance the courageous take in the struggle for justice; therein lies true humility. The most fundamental thing is to have a sense of humility toward the Law and toward truth. It is to our own benefit to advance along the path of faith with sincere humility and a boundless seeking mind. The greater our seeking spirit, the greater the fortune we gain and the stronger and happier we become. (2/16/92)

A vibrant seeking spirit is the very wellspring of Buddhism; the prime point of faith. It is also the great path of the SGI. A person of seeking spirit is always youthful, always full of joy, always vigorous. People with seeking minds humbly examine themselves and strive to develop their lives. Through such efforts, they can develop great character. A genuine Buddhist and genuine member of the SGI always lives vibrantly and continually advances through life with a seeking mind. (4/23/94)

The moment we forget to have a humble seeking mind and instead come to see ourselves as intrinsically great, our ruin begins. This is as true of leaders in the organization as it is of people with social status. (5/3/94)

Buddhism teaches that truly excellent people can learn from everyone, even those on lower levels of development, and they should respect such people, regarding them as their teachers. (2/23/90)

I hope you will always have the spirit to learn with a lively curiosity and interest. When leaders are enthusiastic to keep learning and growing, they inspire others. New ideas emerge and spread. Fresh energy to advance surges forth. Instead of pretending to know all the answers, assuming an air of superior wisdom, let us always strive for greater understanding and insight into all manner of things, so that we continue learning together and spur one another to grow further. This is the kind of spirit I cherish. (4/19/97)

SINCERITY

Our sincere prayers for kosen-rufu reach the Gohonzon on a profound level, thereby activating the protective functions of the Buddhist gods. In the long-range view, a sincere and honest person is always a victor. No matter how circumstances may change, no one can take away the truth in others' hearts. (2/24/90)

Throughout his life, Shakyamuni encouraged people with his clear, sonorous voice. A Buddhist text describes how Shakyamuni warmheartedly welcomed everyone he met, expressing his joy at meeting them. He showed affection, joy and gentleness in all his interactions. He greeted everyone with courtesy and respect. He never scowled or grimaced. To put others at ease and encourage them to speak up, Shakyamuni would always break the ice by initiating conversation. It was the power of Shakyamuni's eloquence and sincerity that made it possible for Buddhism to gain wide acceptance among the people of his time. (1/27/95)

If we are sincere, people will understand our intentions, and our positive qualities will shine forth. It is pointless to be caught up in outward appearances. (DOY 1, ch. 10)

SLANDER

"To speak ill of that person [who embraces the supreme Law] is to speak ill of the Law, just as to show contempt for the son is to show contempt for the parents who bore him" (MW-5, 32). The "person" here, in the specific sense, refers to Nichiren Daishonin. In a broad sense, however, it indicates his followers, we Soka Gakkai members who promote kosen-rufu. To speak ill of those who propagate the Law even at the cost of their lives is to speak ill of the Mystic Law. To show contempt for the children of the Buddha is to show contempt for the Buddha himself. (9/30/91)

When people worship the Gohonzon, all Buddhas and bodhisattvas in the entire universe immediately respond to their prayers by lending their protection. If people slander the Gohonzon, the response will be exactly the opposite. For this reason, one's mind of faith is extremely important. The mind of faith has a subtle and far-reaching influence. (2/27/90)

Shijo Kingo suffered on account of calumny. But the Daishonin told him, "Never let life's hardships disturb you." Those who resort to libelous accusations are defeated as human beings; no action is more lowly and base. We should not be swayed in the least by such despicable actions. Just as we do not put garbage into our mouths, we must not permit such rubbish to enter our hearts. The Daishonin encouraged Shijo Kingo to shut the cowardly behavior of his accusers out of his mind. The Roman philosopher Seneca says that the arrows of slander cannot pierce the heart of a person of wisdom. (LG, p. 242)

Those who abuse the SGI, who exploit the members for their own selfish reasons and aims, are committing the gravest slander of the Law. (6/25/96)

There are cases when we wonder why merit doesn't reveal itself in spite of our earnest and high degree of faith. At such times, rather than suspecting that you may entertain doubt about the Gohonzon, it is better to ask yourself whether you are guilty of any slander. Because a person who is contemptuous, hating, jealous or holds grudges will realize no benefits. (2/20/90)

Buddhism reveals the ultimate Law of the universe and the ultimate principle for achieving happiness. Taking faith in Buddhism plants the seed of true happiness in our lives. Therefore, we must not uproot and throw away, scorch or otherwise spoil this seed of happiness as a result of harboring hatred and jealousy toward fellow believers and eventually discarding our faith. (2/14/90)

STUDY

The purpose of practice is to assist and support faith, and the purpose of study is to support practice. We can also say that practice is led by faith, and that study follows practice. Thus we must not practice in a way that contradicts our faith. And we must not engage in study in a way that it obstructs our practice. (9/16/93)

The Gosho, the collected writings of Nichiren Daishonin, elucidates the means for all people to attain enlightenment. It is the eternal teaching. The Gosho is a scripture of boundless hope. As long as we continue to study the Gosho and put its teachings into practice, we will definitely never become deadlocked. (LG, p. 7)

It is imperative that you have wisdom. For that reason it is vital that, based on chanting daimoku, you study diligently, starting with the Daishonin's teachings. It is essential that you develop and strengthen your intellect. (2/2/93)

The Daishonin's words are guiding principles that have universal, eternal relevance. It is important to study his writings. And it is especially crucial that the members of the youth division gain a grounding in Buddhist study. The two ways of practice and study are both important. A halfhearted attitude will not allow you to complete these two paths. That would be a truly sad thing. (5/26/98)

Education definitely changes people's lives. This is why the SGI is so earnest when it comes to Buddhist study, the highest field of learning; it is the study of human beings and the foremost education. Buddhist study is the soul of the SGI. (1/6/96)

∽

Imagine someone new to the study of physics sitting in on lectures by Einstein, who stood at the pinnacle of his field. If from the outset the neophyte doubted everything Einstein said, he or she would not grow in understanding. Therefore, President Toda taught that when we read the Gosho, we should receive it with our entire beings—with a spirit of "Yes, that's exactly right." This is the shortcut to happiness. (LG, p. 84)

∽

In the clear mirror of the Gosho, the true nature of all things becomes apparent. That is why it is important to hone our wisdom through Buddhist study. (2/24/96)

∽

The Daishonin urges us to earnestly chant Nam-myoho-renge-kyo, even just once or twice, stressing that if we do so we will definitely attain enlightenment. Now some might immediately think, "All right! I'll just put faith aside and take it easy, then embrace faith seriously a year before I die." But the Daishonin's words in this instance are meant to spur his followers to devote greater efforts to their Buddhist practice, emphasizing the beneficial power of chanting even a single daimoku. The correct way to read the Gosho is to always interpret the Daishonin's words from the standpoint of strengthening our faith. (3/24/97)

∽

What is the purpose of study? It's to enable us to gain some practical ability or knowledge so that we can contribute to society and to the happiness and welfare of many people. (DOY 2, ch. 21)

～

Some Gosho, of course, are very doctrinal and complex. But we do not necessarily have to understand all of the Daishonin's writings. The important thing is to have a keen desire to read the Gosho and to expose our lives, even for just a short time each day, to Nichiren Daishonin's spirit. Having such a seeking mind enables us to securely anchor our lives in the orbit of true happiness, in the path of attaining Buddhahood in this lifetime. (LG, p. 7)

～

I hope that each of you will study broadly and develop your understanding of life, society and the universe, based on your faith in Nichiren Daishonin's Buddhism. This type of learning enables you to cultivate a rich state of life, or inner world, drawing forth profound wisdom and limitless leadership ability from the depths of life. (2/14/90)

～

Let's read the Gosho regularly. Even just a little is fine. Even a single sentence. Just opening the Gosho is a start. At any rate, let's strive to read the Daishonin's writings. It's important to have the spirit to study the Gosho, to open up the Gosho. Even if you forget what you've read, something profound will have been engraved in the depths of your life. (3/24/97)

～

The Gosho is the jewel of humankind that crystallizes with diamond-like clarity the humanism of Nichiren Daishonin. Because this is an age of spiritual malaise, it is all the more important that we study the Gosho and return to the humanism of Nichiren Daishonin. (LG, p. 26)

TRUE CAUSE

Mr. Toda once told me: "You can make defeat the cause for future victory. You can also make victory the cause for future defeat." The Buddhism of Nichiren Daishonin is the Buddhism of true cause, the Buddhism of the present and the future. We don't dwell on the past. We are always challenging ourselves from the present toward the future. "The whole future lies ahead of us! We have only just begun!" Because we advance with this spirit, we will never be deadlocked. (12/16/96)

During our dialogue, Dr. Arnold Toynbee at one point told me that his motto was *Laboremus,* Latin for, "Let's get to work!" Nichiren Daishonin's Buddhism focuses on the present and future; it is infused with the spirit, "Let's get started!" We practice for the sake of the present and future. It is important not to become trapped in the past; we have to put the past behind us. The Buddhism of true cause is always based on the present moment; it is always "from this moment on." (3/24/97)

Forward! Always forward! This is a basic spirit of Buddhism. Nichiren Daishonin's teaching is the Buddhism of true cause. We live with our gaze fixed on the future, not hung up on the past. To advance eternally—this is the essence of life and the essence of what it means to be a practitioner of the Daishonin's Buddhism. (7/9/97)

WISDOM

Buddhism is wisdom. As long as we have wisdom, we can put all things to their best use and can turn everything in the direction of happiness. (4/23/96)

~

We live in an age where opportunities for profound life-to-life inspiration are all but nonexistent. Idle amusements bring only fleeting pleasure. They produce neither profound inspiration nor growth for one's life. By contrast, Buddhism exists to enable people to realize personal growth and to improve their lives. Buddhism is always rooted in the reality of life. It is the wellspring of wisdom for bringing harmony and happiness to our families, local communities and society at large. (1/27/96)

~

Faith manifests itself as wisdom. The purpose of our faith is to become wise, so that we can live wisely. (2/3/93)

~

Strong faith enables you to display your wisdom appropriately, so that you can take advantage of change and move forward in the direction of victory and hope. You can definitely show actual proof and benefit in accordance with the Gosho passage "Those who believe in the Lotus Sutra [Gohonzon] will gather fortune from ten thousand miles afar"(MW-1, 272). (1/31/93)

~

Since the Gohonzon is "always here, preaching the Law," by chanting daimoku we can, under any circumstances, gain the wisdom to know the proper course of action. The Daishonin says, "When the skies are clear, the ground is illuminated"

(MW-1, 82). Similarly, when the sun of wisdom rises in our lives, the correct path is illuminated. (LG, p. 43)

In "Letter to Akimoto," the Daishonin states, "If the mind of faith is perfect, then the water of wisdom, the great impartial wisdom, will never dry up" (MW-7, 195). If one has faith, wisdom wells forth. Wisdom is proof of faith. As the expression "great impartial wisdom" indicates, impartiality and fairness are essential requirements of a Buddhist leader. (6/5/96)

Leadership

Behavior

I would like leaders to make efforts so that people will say about them: "That person really put my mind at ease. I was convinced, reassured and encouraged. I now feel more confident and full of hope." Leaders must never give orders or dictate to the members. I hope you will be gentle leaders who are generous in giving reassurance and peace of mind to fellow members. To be strict with oneself but gentle with others—this is the spirit of one who has strong faith. (9/18/93)

Women's division members have remarked that many men resort to scheming and saying things that aren't true. Remember, the women's division members are sharp. They see right through leaders who lie or are cunning; they see through everything. Accordingly, such tactics won't work and should be abandoned. A leader who loses the trust of the women's division is all washed up. The only way to gain their trust is by working sincerely and honestly. (2/24/96)

Leadership is not a matter of ordering people around but of first taking action yourself. By initiating action yourself, you will win others' trust, and they, in turn, will take action. (5/17/95)

I hope that leaders will earnestly pray for the prosperity, safety and happiness of the members who are all so infinitely noble and praiseworthy. May you also never forget to develop yourselves and pray to become people who are liked and trusted by the members, who can work unstintingly for the members' happiness and well-being. (11/23/96)

The leader's role is important. Everything is determined by the leader's behavior. A passage in *The Romance of the Three Kingdoms* says that only those who possess genuine wisdom and virtue can win the highest regard from people. It all comes down to you. You have to polish and develop yourselves. Should there be leaders in faith whom you do not like, all you have to do is determine not to become like them. All you have to do is decide that you will become leaders who make everyone feel comfortable and at ease. (6/5/96)

Attempting to move people to action merely with orders or rallying cries is cold and mechanical; it is not humanism. It is all too easy to deal with others bureaucratically and impersonally. Managing people in this fashion is dangerous. Leaders should not think about becoming great in terms of the organization but as human beings. (12/10/94)

It is important for leaders to have the spirit to bring out each person's potential. Leaders shouldn't judge others based on outward appearances or decide from their own narrow perspective that someone is unsuitable or no good. Racking your brain over how to uncover and bring out others' strong points is the true measure of a leader. This is the art of leadership. (5/17/95)

The safety and well-being of the members are always the first priority. It is the duty of leaders to protect the members. No matter what anyone might say, I will always stand by the members. I live for their sake. I hope that all of you share this spirit. (2/25/95)

One should avoid prejudging people at all costs. Any person we meet may be an outstanding individual who possesses tremendous potential of which we have no inkling. (2/26/90)

What lengths the Daishonin went to for his followers! In his actions we see his spirit to protect resolutely all who embrace the Mystic Law, his determination for the well-being of all his followers, and his firm conviction: "If I don't protect them, who will?" Through his example, it seems to me, the Daishonin teaches the proper attitude for all Buddhist leaders. (LG, p. 166)

How deplorable is the arrogance of authoritarian leaders! On the reverse side of such arrogance lies cowardice—a lack of courage to see the truth. Likewise, discrimination and envy are also two sides of the same coin. (1/26/96)

A leader is not one who stands above others, much less one who declares "I am special" and regards others with contempt. The moment one resolves to join in and work alongside everyone, to respect everyone and have the spirit to humbly learn from them, one embarks on the road to becoming a great leader. This was also one of the essential points of the "leadership revolution" of which President Makiguchi spoke. (6/23/96)

∽

The following are some important guidelines for leaders: Create an environment where each person wants to take leadership and responsibility. Learn yourself and encourage others to do the same. This process of continual learning by all parties is the key to success. Realize that constructive change in your organization begins when you, the leader, change first. (6/23/96)

CARE OF MEMBERS

It is important for leaders to love people, to treasure everyone. To the extent that we love others, we will be loved. To the extent that we work for others' happiness, we will enjoy protection and support. This is the law of cause and effect. It is also the path for developing our humanity. (Dialogue 6, 1994)

∽

Our fellow members are all family with whom we are linked by deep bonds. If we support and protect this family, they will act as protective forces in our environment, supporting and keeping us from harm lifetime after lifetime. This is a profound principle of Buddhism. (4/19/97)

∽

I hope that all of you will work with all your might to ensure that each member without fail comes to shine with happiness as bright and complete as the full moon. Please pursue sincere and patient dialogue that will both encourage your members and deeply touch their hearts. With warm concern and kindness, please treasure each person with all your heart and make your organization shine with an even greater harmonious unity as sublime as the full moon itself. (6/6/96)

Please make every effort to find and raise capable people. My wish is that you construct a wonderful organization, joyfully building growing spheres of friendship and a solidarity of people who cherish hope for life and the future. (7/3/96)

Even if all the leaves on a tree should fall off in a strong wind, as long as the branches and trunk remain intact, in time the tree will again produce flowers. Likewise, the spread of Buddhism will continue as long as there remain people of genuine faith. The important thing, therefore, is to raise one person of genuine faith. (LG, p. 128)

Capable people are the greatest treasure. Without capable people neither the eternal establishment of the Law nor kosen-rufu can be achieved. First of all, you must "find" capable people. Just as a miner searches for gold ore in ordinary rocks, you have to look for members who possess great potential and then work to develop their ability with your heart and soul. (2/13/90)

Prayer is most fundamental in raising capable people. You pray earnestly to the Gohonzon that the person you have found will become an able person important to the SGI–USA. And then, with this prayer, you take the utmost care to help that person develop. (2/13/90)

You should sincerely respect capable people and raise them with the determination to make them more outstanding and more able than you are yourself. Looking down on one's juniors or exploiting them for personal gain is an offense comparable to that of slandering the Law. Please remember that one who raises capable people is great. Such a person is truly capable and important. (2/13/90)

There may be some members who work at night or have irregular working hours and others who are extremely busy with work. Such people might find it difficult to attend meetings. But they are also challenging their individual problems and trying hard to show actual proof of faith. I want you to become considerate leaders who can understand others' situations. (2/25/90)

"How can I help others experience joy? How can I help them practice in high spirits and really exert themselves?" It goes without saying that someone who gives no thought to these questions and does not respond to members' needs is not qualified to be a leader in the humane world of Buddhism. Therefore, our practice has to be based on strong prayer for the happiness of each person. (LG, p. 153)

A single individual is important. Everything starts from treasuring just one person. This is the eternal formula for the development of kosen-rufu. (6/15/96)

Leaders must love the members as if they were their own children. They, more than anyone else, must pray for their members' happiness. In this single thought for the members'

happiness lies all the power needed for development. From this compassion springs the wisdom to bring hope and joy to others. (2/5/93)

Why have we, the SGI, achieved such remarkable development? Because we have wholeheartedly treasured each individual member as a child of the Buddha, in exact accord with this compassionate spirit of the Daishonin. (1/27/93)

DIALOGUE

A report from The Club of Rome in 1992 stated that a leader should possess "effectiveness in taking decisions after due dialogue with colleagues and advisers, in ensuring the implementation of the decisions and, in due time, in assessing the results." Dialogue and action—it is important that these be employed simultaneously. We take action while holding discussions and discuss things while taking action. Herein lies the strength of the SGI's tradition. (5/12/92)

After fully hearing out the views of everyone, one should judge things impartially and come to a decision. And once one has done so, one should rise to implement it without vacillation. Please make united efforts that demonstrate responsiveness to others' views. (5/12/92)

Commands or expressions like "must" or "have to" no longer motivate people in this day and age. This is a time in which no one will act unless they are truly convinced in their hearts. On the other hand, when someone is truly moved, he may display his great potential, showing tremendous power and ability. For this reason, fruitful conferences and discussions are becoming all the more important, while one-to-one dialogue is becoming tremendously vital. (12/12/87)

I can not emphasize enough the importance of dialogue, for I believe that the propensity for logic and discussion is the proof of one's humanity. In other words, only when we are immersed in an ocean of language do we become truly human. (1/26/89)

Frank and sincere discussion is what opens up a person's heart. When you continue this kind of friendly dialogue with someone, things naturally and inevitably turn to faith. (3/22/89)

It is necessary to have the strength to strictly argue and refute anyone who disparages the Law. However, a person will not be able to gain the heartfelt agreement of others by ability alone. It often happens that the level of discussion will become more profound and your negation of false assertions more convincing when you listen attentively to, and show understanding for, what the other person has to say. (7/14/89)

To whomever you are speaking, if you have a broad mind and the magnanimous spirit to embrace and understand their feelings, their hearts will open up, revealing understanding and sympathy. Your ability to do this depends on your state of your life. If you develop a state of life that enables you to be flexible, you can easily open the door to other people's hearts, stirring or soothing their emotions, developing on the situation.

This is the essence of a dialogue based on a profound understanding of human nature. (7/14/89)

Mr. Toda spoke candidly and vigorously with anyone, creating a history of dialogue with people from all walks of life—from ordinary citizens to government ministers. Only human beings can fill society and the world with dialogue. Dialogue has the power to produce great value, irrespective of the wealth or social position of participants. I, too, have conducted dialogue with countless people; the eminent persons or dignitaries with whom I have met number as many as 2,000. This is my history and the history of kosen-rufu. (6/20/90)

Small-scale discussions or dialogues are important, the kind where you can talk directly, face to face, close enough to sense each other's warmth. Discussion that is not unilateral but convincing—discussion carried out in this way can revive weary hearts, open closed minds and change the cycle of bewilderment and despair into one of conviction and hope. (6/1/91)

Where there is an atmosphere of lively discussion, where people can say or ask anything, it is bright and joyful. In such an environment there is growth. The rhythm of kosen-rufu, of moving forward, is there. (LG, p. 76)

A leader must always make the effort and have the latitude to listen to each person's opinion. One who can humbly listen to the words of another is wise. A good leader understands the power of dialogue. He or she tenaciously works to create a venue and to make time for discussion. By contrast, a leader who fears and seeks to avoid person-to-person dialogue is going against the times. More likely than not, such a leader is self-complacent and tyrannical in disposition. (5/12/92)

What is the most important point in conducting dialogue? It is to be a good listener. Though seemingly simple, listening well is actually quite difficult. The ancient Greek philosopher Zeno said, "Two ears to one tongue, therefore hear twice as much as you speak." It is often the case that just being able to share one's problems with someone else is all it takes to put a person's troubled mind at ease. The Chinese character for "ear" is central to the meaning of the characters for "wise" and "sage." A person who listens well is wise; and the wisest of the wise is the sage. (6/10/91)

Through our efforts at dialogue, through our actions, we are fundamentally changing a society that lacks compassion and is awash with false friendship. We are transforming the destiny of our society, which tends to be discriminatory and lacking in compassion. We are sending the sunlight of spring to a society locked in a frigid winter. We are thawing people's hearts with a warm current of humanity. (LG, p. 57)

Let us do our utmost to sustain the wonderfully warm atmosphere of the SGI—an atmosphere where members feel free to discuss whatever is on their minds. Unless we do so, our organization will stop growing, stop developing. The SGI is a world of humanity—of the heart, of faith, of compassion. It is a world of unity and mutual inspiration. That is why it is strong. If we continue to value and promote these qualities, the SGI will continue to grow and develop forever. I want to declare here and now the atmosphere where we can discuss anything is fundamental to the SGI. (6/16/98)

This spirit of engaging others in dialogue on equal terms is the essence of Buddhism. Ordering people about in a high-handed, arrogant manner, shouting at them to do one's bidding is truly deplorable behavior. Such a world has no relation to Buddhism. Through dialogue Shakyamuni opened hearts that were closed, softened hearts that had grown hard and melted hearts that were frozen. (1/27/96)

ENCOURAGEMENT

The main point in giving guidance is to elevate the *ichinen* (determination) of the other person. A change in your *ichinen* will cause a change in the prayers that you offer and the actions that you take. According to the doctrine of *ichinen sanzen* (3,000 realms in a single moment of life), subtle and imperceptible changes in your *ichinen* affect everything immensely. One who can help raise another person's *ichinen* is an outstanding leader. Those who merely issue orders or give directions—to say nothing of those who just scold and lord it over others—do not qualify as leaders. (9/23/91)

From the standpoint of faith, to keep silent when one sees something amiss is tantamount to lacking mercy. Although to criticize and censure someone out of petty emotionalism is of course incorrect, it is necessary that constructive and valuable opinions be aired. If a leader is broad-minded enough to listen with a sense of appreciation, both he and the person sharing his views can expand their state of life. (2/21/90)

I hope all of you will attain excellence in giving individual guidance and become "excellent doctors" of human existence and life's inner dynamics. The human heart is very vulnerable. You should continually ask yourself: How can I give others confidence and enable them to advance with courage and strong determination? (9/23/91)

∽

Problems that arise are many and diverse, varying from person to person and from one situation to the next. And people have greatly differing characters. For this reason, to give effective guidance, you yourselves must accumulate rich experience, develop your understanding of Buddhism and polish your faith. I hope you will lead others with wisdom, all the while praying for their happiness with the spirit of compassion. (9/23/91)

∽

In the SGI organization, the success of our activities or meetings, for example, hinges on whether the leaders have prayed thoroughly to give each person hope and for each participant, without fail, to leave the activity with a sense of profound fulfillment. Those who are only concerned with what others think of them are not qualified to be SGI leaders. (LG, p. 91)

∽

The main point is to enable one member to stand up by imparting heartfelt assurance and understanding. It is the explosion of faith in the microcosm of an individual that causes the macrocosm of the organization—a gathering of many such individuals—to commence its revolution. This is how the doctrine of 3,000 realms in a single moment of life applies to our practice. (2/15/90)

∽

As SGI leaders, how we interpret the words of members and what we say in response are important. A genuine leader is someone who gives measured thought to such matters. When talking with individuals, ask yourselves: "What are they worried about?" "What are they trying to say?" "What are they thinking? "What is it they seek?" Try to discern these things in others. Try to know. Try to understand. This is the challenge of leadership. From such compassion arises wisdom. (7/16/98)

In giving guidance, leaders must continually ask themselves, "What can I say to this person right now to lift his or her spirits?" "How can I encourage, what can I do to enable this friend to advance with new vitality?" It is important to have this spirit of concern. There is no value in giving one-sided guidance that does not take into account what the other person is thinking or feeling. (2/24/96)

Guidance in Buddhism is aimed at the very depths of life. It is an all-out challenge to motivate people to change their lives. Unless our own lives overflow with vitality, nothing we do or say will penetrate others' lives. (5/17/95)

Above all, the Daishonin did not blithely brandish theories of karma. Making condescending pronouncements to suffering people like "That's just your karma" will only add to their misery. Someone battling destiny feels like there is a gale raging through his or her heart. When we encounter people in such a state, we should stand with them in the rain, become sopping wet with them and work with them to find a way out of the storm. In the end, that's probably all another human being can do. (LG, p. 159)

We each function as a good friend toward one another. To function in this way toward one another it is important to possess a broad heart and mind that can encompass or embrace another person. It is naturally a fundamental principle of faith to give guidance correctly and appropriately. In this respect, it is not wise to offer detailed direction with regard to personal matters or to criticize or lay blame on a person for his particular lifestyle. People have different natures and different ways of living. Their lifestyles and circumstances also differ. It is vitally important to mutually respect and be on good terms with one another. (12/12/87)

It is important to have the compassion to respond to a person's needs and situation, to give considered thought to how you can best help him or her and then take appropriate action. Wisdom arises from compassion. (2/24/96)

It is no good to give uniform, one-sided guidance. All laws are part of the Buddhist Law. The universe itself and all phenomena are Buddhism. Therefore, we have to consider things from a lofty and broad perspective. The point is to be flexible and to use one's wisdom to make everyone feel invigorated. To be able to give such encouragement is a sign of strong faith in the truest sense of the term. (2/24/96)

In any struggle, the critical point is how a leader inspires others. As you are leaders of kosen-rufu, I ask that you encourage friends of the Mystic Law in such a manner that the powers of faith and life force surge forth in their lives. I hope that your efforts in the struggle of faith will serve to increase the majesty and strength of the Buddhist gods. (2/14/90)

If individuals are manipulated to serve the needs of an organization and its leadership, the spirit of Buddhism is contradicted. In Buddhism, such a perverse relationship between the organization or leadership and the individual will block the flow of benefits and stifle the development of kosen-rufu. Giving warm encouragement and care to each person is the basis for victory. (2/15/90)

If a person is hungry, we should give them bread. When there is no bread, we can at least give words that nourish. To a person who looks ill or is physically frail, we can turn the conversation to some subject that will lift their spirits and fill them with the hope and determination to get better. Let us give something to each person we meet: joy, courage, hope, assurance, or philosophy, wisdom, a vision for the future. Let us always give something. (12/16/96)

Encouragement—offering encouraging words—is important. Nichiren Daishonin states, "The voice does the Buddha's work" (*Gosho Zenshu,* p. 708). Sincere words of encouragement have the power to give people hope and courage to go on living. (1/27/95)

We use our voices not only to chant daimoku but to guide, encourage and introduce others to the Daishonin's Buddhism. Our voice, therefore, is very important. An angry voice, a coarse voice, a cold voice, an imperious voice—none of these will communicate how wonderful Nichiren Daishonin's Buddhism is. I would like you to be humanistic leaders who can encourage others with bright warm voices, so that they will say, "What a lovely voice!" and "I'm always so inspired when

I hear you speak." Becoming this kind of leader is one actual proof of your human revolution. (5/23/96)

Our voice costs nothing and it is our strongest weapon. Nichiren Daishonin wrote, "Do not spare your voice" (*Gosho Zenshu,* p. 726). There are different voices for different situations: the clear, resounding voice that declares truth and justice; the strong voice that refutes evil; the bright, confident voice that tells others about the greatness of this Buddhism; the warm voice that gives encouragement; the sincere, friendly voice that offers praise and words of appreciation to others. The important thing is that we meet and speak with people widely, inside and outside the organization. (11/17/96)

Our voice costs nothing and it is our strongest weapon.

No one can hold a candle to those who have devoted themselves to caring for others, who have offered ceaseless encouragement to their friends. Such people lead the most noble and respectable lives—lives like a magnificent Hawaiian sunset. (1/27/93)

GROWTH

As leaders, I hope you will study ceaselessly and strive to deepen your character and refinement. At the same time, I would like you to be people brimming with a genuine and unpretentious humanity. (6/6/96)

If leaders make constant efforts to study hard, grow and maintain a sense of freshness, the organization will advance and be filled with dynamism. An organization will change and develop only to the extent that leaders change and develop themselves. The advancement of kosen-rufu in the community and country proceeds likewise. (2/19/90)

⌒

Leaders must study continually. Once a leader stops growing, those who look to him or her for guidance and support will suffer. (6/6/96)

⌒

Leaders who are responsible for organizing and holding discussion meetings in the SGI must study. If they do not, they cannot hope to satisfy the participants and inspire them with fresh energy and enthusiasm. (7/19/96)

⌒

When leaders, owing to arrogance or decadence, cease to develop, the organization that they head falls to ruin. This is a basic principle of history, an unchanging truth in all ages. (12/10/94)

NURTURING YOUTH

When youth are awakened to a sense of mission, their power is limitless. Ultimately, we have to entrust our hopes and visions for the future to the youth. This is a golden rule. Youth is pure. Youth will rise up to fulfill their ideals without calculation or self-interest. The fundamental spirit of a leader must be to reach out to such young people, work with them and bring out their capabilities and direct their youthful energies in a positive direction. (3/5/97)

⌒

Toward a member of the young men's division or student division, for example, rather than discussing difficult issues, it may sometimes be more inspiring to say something like, "You must be hungry. Why don't we go down to the corner and grab a bite to eat. I'll treat you." Or, to a young women's division member who is discouraged because she is making little headway in activities for kosen-rufu, you might say something like, "Please don't worry. I'll do it for you." Addressing people in this way can give them great peace of mind. After all, for people to merely possess the spirit to want to work for kosen-rufu is in itself a wonderful thing. (2/24/96)

Something that characterizes true leaders is that they are thoroughly dedicated to raising young people. When you put all of your energy into developing the rich potential of youth, both you and the organization are rejuvenated. I hope that you will find and raise people with great potential, allowing them to steadily rise and fully engage themselves. If you create such a flow, the future will open up boundlessly before you. (2/21/90)

Let us care for and nurture the members of the youth and future divisions. My prayer is that each of you will foster your juniors to become even more capable than yourself, while striving ceaselessly for your own self-improvement so that you may bring your life to a wonderful completion. (6/23/96)

Nobel laureate Gabriela Mistral (1889–1957) of Chile, was well respected as a humanistic educator. Indicative of the great spirit of compassion and caring with which she interacted with her students is her "Teacher's Prayer": "Let me be more mother than the mother herself in my love and defense of the child who is not flesh of my flesh. Help me to make one of my children my most perfect poem and leave within him or her my most melodious melody from that day when my own lips no longer sing." With this same spirit, let us care for and nurture young people. (6/23/96)

Rosa Parks, the highly respected civil rights activist, said that she derives her greatest pleasure from working with and for youth. Let us, too, joyfully and wholeheartedly exert ourselves in the task of nurturing the messengers of the future, our precious youth. (2/3/93)

POSITION

Leaders, in particular, tend to become arrogant just because they hold high positions in the organization and think that they know everything. This is a common tendency. They put on airs and regard other truly upright people as being below them. This kind of behavior only alienates people. It also destroys the leader's own good fortune. To leaders, I would like to say: The higher your position in the organization, the stronger should be your desire to learn from everyone around you. (9/18/93)

We must never allow the slightest trace of discrimination to enter our sphere of endeavors. We are all equal as human beings. In the eyes of the Mystic Law, all members—leaders and nonleaders alike—are equal. This is the Buddhism of Nichiren Daishonin and the world of the Soka family. (9/26/93)

Leadership positions in the organization are, after all, just a bunch of made-up titles. Faith is what is crucial. No matter what leadership position one may occupy, without faith, there will be no benefit. It is the same as quitting one's practice. Such leaders are simply taking advantage of the Soka Gakkai and the members' sincere faith. (DOY 2, ch. 21)

Organizational position and social standing do not make anyone superior. We are all fellow members—comrades striving together toward the same goal. The SGI is a community of people who respect one another and work together to realize world peace. (2/24/96)

The fundamental spirit of Buddhism is that all people are equal. A person is not great simply because of his or her social standing, fame, academic background or position in the organization. In the world of faith, the truly great are those who spread the Mystic Law and strive for kosen-rufu, who actively work for the sake of Buddhism and the happiness of others. Supremely respectworthy are those who champion the cause of kosen-rufu. (1/8/98)

Buddhism is an all-out, earnest struggle. There is no place in Buddhist practice for an easygoing or lackadaisical attitude. Having a position in the organization or social standing does not mean we can automatically give others hope. Only by waging a great inner struggle, with the spirit to expend our very lives, can we truly encourage others. (LG, p. 165)

All people are equal. There are absolutely no distinctions of superior and inferior among human beings. Differences of position in an organization are temporary and provisional. They are no more than an expedient means for enabling all members to practice joyfully and become truly happy. (2/21/90)

In our organization, there is no one above or below; everyone is equal. The higher one's leadership position, the more humbly and respectfully one must work for the happiness of the members. This is how genuine Buddhist leaders behave. (6/6/96)

At a crucial moment it is the strength and courage of ordinary people who have no name or position in society that save the day. The famous, the well-connected, almost always have too much to lose, and they abandon the cause in order to protect themselves. (3/18/97)

Position and appearances are irrelevant. The important thing is to carry out our personal duty, our commitment, no matter what anyone else may say. This is a life of true victory, a life of unsurpassed nobility and fulfillment. (3/18/98)

A true leader is someone who protects his members, praising them and being tolerant toward them. In contrast, leaders who exploit their positions in the organization, rebuking people and acting in a high-handed manner, not only cause the Buddha's children to suffer but make causes for their own suffering in the future as well. (2/12/90)

PRAISE AND APPRECIATION

Sometimes members cannot be on time to certain meetings or cannot come at all. No one in the organization has the right to scold a person in this kind of situation. On the contrary, leaders should warmly welcome such members. A true family is pervaded by a spirit of praise and encouragement for individual members' sincere efforts. (2/25/90)

As a specific point for leaders to bear in mind, it is important that you praise and encourage your fellow members. You must never direct your anger toward others out of emotion, shouting at or abusing them. In the Gosho, the Daishonin cites the words of the Great Teacher Dengyo, who said, "One who praises [the practitioners of the Lotus Sutra] accumulates good fortune as high as Mount Sumeru; one who slanders [them] commits an offense that will lead to the hell of incessant suffering" (*Gosho Zenshu,* p. 1039). (6/23/96)

The most important thing is to offer praise. Being human, people experience various ups and downs in their emotional state. So I'd like to see leaders offering encouragement and heartfelt praise to those they encounter—even simply remarking brightly, "Thank you!" or "I really appreciate all your efforts!" Both parties will then feel cheered and refreshed. Ripples of joy will spread out to others and all will enjoy that much more benefit. (6/26/96)

I hope that as leaders you will always express your appreciation for and do your utmost to support the many sincere members who are steadfastly exerting themselves in faith. The Daishonin says that when you see someone who embraces the Mystic Law, you should rise and greet them from afar, showing them the same respect you would a Buddha. (4/21/98)

Our heart is what matters most. A heart that praises the Mystic Law brings forth boundless benefit. And the heart that praises those who spread the Mystic Law elicits still greater benefit. I hope all the leaders in the SGI will have a spirit to praise others and put everyone at ease, creating a warm and pleasant atmosphere. Kosen-rufu expands where people feel a true sense of pleasure and enjoyment. (6/14/96)

QUALITIES OF LEADERS

Leaders in faith need to possess unshakable confidence in the Mystic Law, a warm sensitivity and thoughtfulness, and the ability to respond to the hearts of others with wisdom and flexibility. Without such qualities, they cannot hope to win the trust of many people or realize kosen-rufu. Conversely, the more there are leaders who do possess such qualities, the more our kosen-rufu movement will advance. (2/24/96)

A leader doesn't have to be anyone special, just a person who values and respects all people equally. A leader who is not one of the people will not be able to understand their hearts. A person bereft of simple humanity will not understand others' feelings. No matter how high their positions, leaders have to remain of the people. While this may seem an unremarkable observation, this is an essential requirement of a democratic leader. (3/17/95)

First, never be haughty. Leaders must be modest through and through.

Second, never reprimand others. You should always treat others gently. In the Gosho we find the statement, "He makes it possible for the offender to rid himself of evil, and thus he acts like a parent to the offender" (MW-2, 211). Naturally it will sometimes be necessary for you to admonish or encourage others with a spirit of compassion. But you must not scold people in a fit of emotion.

Third, never raise your voice with fellow members. Leaders should be people of reason who always seek to win others' understanding through discussion.

Fourth, do not lie. Because we are common mortals, we make mistakes. There is no reason to feel that we have to cover up these errors. The world of faith is a world where things can be discussed frankly, without any concealment. Honest people will win the trust of those around them.

Fifth, never betray the privacy of another individual. In the organization, leaders are often called upon to counsel members with personal problems. Those who betray this trust and fail to safeguard individual privacy demonstrate irresponsibility as leaders, as people of faith and as human beings. Leaders must be discreet, sincere people who respect the rights of others.

Sixth, do not look down on others. Leaders who have an inflated sense of self-importance, who look down on and discriminate against others, will eventually reach an impasse in life. All people are equally precious, regardless of their position. Excellent leaders are those who have a heartfelt respect for everyone.

Seventh, do not be unfair. All of the members—whether rich or poor, prominent or lacking in social standing—are irreplaceable children of the Buddha. I hope all of you will become impartial and just leaders.

Eighth, never overly strain yourselves or force members to push themselves beyond reasonable limits. You cannot maintain such a pace for very long. Pushing yourselves too hard is not necessarily a reflection of strong faith. Members can fully display their abilities only if they are allowed a certain amount of latitude.

The last two items I want to mention are included in the qualifications I have just outlined.

Ninth, do not be arrogant. Arrogance undermines humanity and destroys faith.

Tenth, do not be unkind. Spiteful leaders make members miserable. On the other hand, those who can warmly support their juniors—to the point of enabling their juniors to eventually surpass even themselves in ability—are great leaders. (10/2/91)

I hope you will become leaders who possess common sense, sophistication, conviction, sympathy and the spirit to encourage others. I hope you will be people who have warm affection for others, able to share their sorrows and pains; who are brimming with confidence and can instill hope and courage in others; who are always vivacious and who give an indescribable sense of peace of mind and courage to those they meet. With leaders such as this, members can carry out vigorous activities and realize prodigious growth. (10/2/91)

Both speeches made by leaders and the format of meetings should not become monotonous. Great leaders are flexible, broad-minded and innovative; they put people thoroughly at ease and inspire trust and confidence in them. (1/27/93)

You must not be leaders who are like a dried-up, barren wasteland. Such people can shout themselves hoarse, crying "Advance, advance," but when they turn around to look behind them, they'll probably find that no one's following! Please be leaders who possess both charm and wisdom. (1/27/93)

~

Leaders need to have immense wisdom, compassion and courage. Nonetheless, each person is different. There are some who may have an outstanding intellect, others who may possess deep compassion for others, and still others who are filled with courage. Through the Mystic Law, the different strong points of each person come to be used to the fullest to create the greatest possible value. (6/6/96)

~

If, blinded by the "mirage" of an organization, a leader tries to operate by giving orders and applying pressure, nothing will change, because no spontaneous or genuine power will be generated among the people that make up that body. We must understand the subtle character of people's hearts. (2/15/90)

~

The most important condition for leaders is sincerity. By contrast, an authoritarian air will only serve to alienate people, and intelligence alone may not produce anything of lasting value. Sincerity is what touches people's hearts, forges bonds of trust, and imparts a sense of security. A person of sincerity creates a relaxed, almost springlike atmosphere about him or her. (2/21/90)

~

All of you who shoulder the future of the new SGI-USA should be warm and compassionate leaders who thoroughly respect and cherish each individual member. I hope you will be wise leaders who can activate the unlimited potential known as Buddhahood in each person's life and help him or her become even more capable and happier than yourselves. (1/27/93)

In a general sense, the sovereign, teacher and parent might be thought of—to put it in modern terms—as the three necessary attributes of leaders. The virtue of the sovereign lies in protecting people; this corresponds to an unwavering sense of responsibility. The virtue of the teacher lies in guiding people; this is the shining wisdom to guide people along the path of happiness. And the virtue of the parent lies in lovingly raising people; this is a warm, if strict, compassion. (LG, p. 61)

Leaders must have the ability to provide training, protection, guidance and instruction. When someone has a problem, they need to provide kind guidance as well as necessary instruction. By so doing, they can ensure that people do not become deadlocked. (LG, p. 63)

A genuine leader protects people when they are tired, and nurtures them by providing training appropriate to their levels of development. If people are given strict training under circumstances that require protection instead, they will go under. And if they are protectively coddled when instead they need guidance, they will stop growing. (LG, p. 63)

RESPONSIBILITY

The antithesis of the virtue of the sovereign is irresponsibility. We have leaders who carry on in a self-aggrandizing and highhanded manner but who avoid addressing difficult issues, using the rationale that "someone else will take care of it" or that "things will somehow work themselves out." They order other people around and then try to shirk responsibility. Even though they may have the appearance of leaders, they do not qualify as such. They lack the requisite virtue. (LG, p. 61)

A true leader must pay attention to details. Such a meticulous attitude reflects a genuine sense of responsibility. Leaders who are careless and lack compassion, who merely give orders and issue directives, cause suffering for everyone. A leader who becomes self-centered is no longer qualified to be a Buddhist, let alone a leader. (4/2/95)

A sense of responsibility, wisdom and compassion—are not these the most important qualities for leaders, and for all people, to possess? If even a few more leaders possessed these three attributes, it would contribute immensely to easing tension and the general happiness of humankind. But the fact of the matter is that the tendency of all too many leaders in society is just the opposite. (LG, p. 61)

The most important point regarding central figures is that they base themselves on faith in the Gohonzon. If the central figure forgets this vital point and tries to skillfully control and direct the members by exerting authority, there results a very dangerous situation. Such a person could even destroy the beautiful world of the True Law. Therefore, we must always watch that central figures base themselves on and cherish the Law above all else. (2/28/90)

The verse section of the "Life Span" chapter of the Lotus Sutra reads: "At all times I think to myself: / How can I cause living beings / to gain entry into the unsurpassed way / and quickly acquire the body of a Buddha?" (LS16, 232). We who have embraced the Gohonzon should struggle to thoroughly protect all the people in our communities and organizations—to help them become happy, stand up and receive benefit. We should do so with the spirit of this passage, "At all times I think to myself...." Everything depends on leaders having such a sense of responsibility. (LG, p. 175)

"I want to close off the path leading to hell." This was the spirit with which Josei Toda declared his opposition to the use of nuclear weapons: "Anyone who threatens the right to live is a devil, a Satan and a monster." To resolutely close off the path to war and open up the path to peace—this is the virtue of the sovereign and the responsibility of leaders. (LG, p. 63)

The Soka Gakkai's second president, Josei Toda, once said: "All of you gathered here today are Soka Gakkai leaders. Becoming happy yourself is no great challenge; it's quite simple. Working for the happiness of others in addition to your own happiness, however, is the foundation of faith." I think that unless you honestly pray to the Gohonzon to be able to do this, strengthen your faith, and devote yourself to faith with a spirit to seek nothing for yourself, you cannot be called a true leader. (6/23/96)

Everything ultimately depends on whether there is someone who is willing to wage a desperate all-out struggle, someone who will take 100 percent responsibility without relying on or leaving things to others, someone who will work with selfless dedication for the sake of the people without any concern for what others think. Such a person is a true leader and a genuine Buddhist. (10/25/96)

Selfless Dedication

A leader in an organization is not someone who stands above others but one whose role is to serve and support everyone else. This is something that the Soka Gakkai's second president, Josei Toda, used to explain by saying, "Leaders are servants of the members." In a sense, a true leader of kosen-rufu is one who is determined to sacrifice himself for the sake of the members. (2/21/90)

In his *Soka Kyoikugaku Taikei* (System of Value-Creating Pedagogy), founding Soka Gakkai president Tsunesaburo Makiguchi called for a "leadership revolution"—a revolution in our understanding and practice of leadership. He stressed the need for humanity to bring a close to an age where those in positions of power and authority use people as a means to fulfill self-serving ends. It is imperative, he said, that we produce a steady stream of new leaders who will give selflessly of themselves to contribute to people's happiness and welfare. (6/23/96)

The second Soka Gakkai president, Josei Toda, used to spend the early morning hours in contemplation. It is important for leaders to think. They must constantly consider: "What is the best thing for everyone's sake? What do I need to do right now?" To respond to each situation merely on the spur of the moment is dangerous and irresponsible. It also displays a lack of compassion. (Dialogue 1, 1994)

Earnest people will not follow leaders who are not seriously challenging themselves. (2/28/90)

There is nothing tragic or pathetic about selfless devotion. What it essentially means is to discard egoism and selfishness. Some people are quick to complain about the organization or about their fellow members. But true Buddhist practice is never egoistic. Our commitment should be such that even if we should be forced to go to prison for our beliefs, we would do so without complaint. This is because we are the ultimate and prime beneficiaries of our practice. All of our efforts in the sphere of faith bring us closer to attaining Buddhahood. (8/27/97)

A leader's commitment can make all the difference. It is the determination and faith of a single person that can bring out the hidden potential of many and inspire them to unite toward victory. (2/25/96)

Is a leader taking action for the members' happiness and for kosen-rufu, or, conversely, is he or she using the SGI and the members for selfish ends? The difference in commitment, or *ichinen*, may now be invisible. But with the passing of time, it will become manifest with unmistakable clarity. (6/23/96)

STRUGGLE

The Soka Gakkai's second president, Josei Toda, often said: "I lost my beloved wife. I lost my beloved child. That's why I can be president." Someone who has not had to struggle in life, someone for whom everything has gone favorably and as they desired, cannot help others become happy. Unless we have suffered ourselves, we cannot truly understand other people's feelings or the real power of Buddhism. (2/24/96)

Even in times of hardship, the important thing is for each of us to determine that we are the star, the protagonist and hero of our life and to keep moving forward. Putting ourselves down and shrinking back from obstacles looming before us spell certain defeat. Through making ourselves strong and developing our state of life, we can definitely find a way. As long as we uphold the Mystic Law throughout our lives, we can break through any impasse and surmount any obstacle. We will also be able to lead all those who are suffering to happiness. (2/24/96)

THOUGHTFULNESS

Leaders should not needlessly give members a hard time. Scolding a member who is sincerely doing activities amounts to the offense of holding a fellow believer in contempt, one of the fourteen slanders. (2/25/90)

Remembering things about a person is an expression of compassion and concern. Forgetfulness shows a lack of compassion, a lack of responsibility. (4/6/98)

Mencius (c. 371–289 B.C.), a great Confucian philosopher who ranks alongside Confucius, observes: "The people will delight in the joy of him who delights in their joy." That is, if a leader rejoices in the happiness of the people, the people, in turn, will rejoice in that leader's happiness. (6/6/96)

~

There are some male leaders who are lax and permissive toward their wives and children but very strict toward others. This is not a good attitude, and to conduct oneself in such a manner is a serious mistake. To coddle those in one's own family while scolding women's division members, treating one's fellow members as though they were underlings; to take good care of one's own home while being thoughtless in the use of another's—this conduct is impermissible and should not be tolerated. (2/24/96)

~

If leaders in faith go on talking for a long time when the other person is hungry, or if they simply parrot words like, "Go for it! Up and at 'em!" to someone who is feeling under the weather, their words will not be received well, even by someone with a positive attitude. (2/24/96)

~

It is natural to encourage the person standing right in front of you. However, the true worth of leaders is determined by the extent to which they direct their attention toward those supporting that person at home or behind the scenes. Behind each individual is a network of connections with many others, including family members and friends. What is important is how much consideration we can show toward these people. (12/10/94)

~

We must not allow ourselves to become bureaucratic and take for granted the efforts of those working behind the scenes. Nor must we ever forget to be considerate of those

members of our families who may not be practicing the Daishonin's Buddhism. We must remember that for every person
involved in SGI activities there is another supporting him or
her behind the scenes. (3/20/96)

A leader is one who causes people to feel joy. The mission of
a leader is to encourage people and elevate their spirits. A
leader absolutely must not scold others. Nothing qualifies a
leader to castigate a friend. (LLS-1, p. 124)

Our Treasured Organization

ACTIVITIES

The royal path of our human revolution lies in the ongoing process of developing ourselves and helping others to develop. In this sense, our activities might be thought of as a movement to expand the mind, the inner realm of life, and the humanism of ourselves and others. (Dialogue 1, 1994)

By steadily continuing to exert ourselves in SGI activities, we will definitely enter the orbit of good fortune. Especially when we endeavor to do our very best in such activities despite our many commitments, all the greater will be the tail wind of good fortune that propels us forward. How wonderful this is! What a profound existence we can lead! (3/8/96)

We could liken doing gongyo and chanting daimoku to the Earth's rotation on its axis, while taking part in activities resembles the Earth's revolution around the sun. To enter this orbit, which enables us to savor a state where life is an unparalleled joy, is itself proof of our attainment of Buddhahood. In the present age, SGI activities represent the means by which we can attain Buddhahood. (3/8/96)

It is important to push ourselves to advance on the forefront. It all comes down to self-motivation, conviction and the spirit to stand alone. Those who do activities only because they are told to do so, or out of a sense of obligation, will not experience true joy. (LG, p. 197)

~

Kosen-rufu is a very long struggle. It is a march that will continue over the 10,000 years of the Latter Day of the Law. Therefore, let us advance joyfully and unhurriedly. Activities must not be conducted in such a way that people suffer and become exhausted. Meetings should be short and not too numerous, conducted so that they are valuable and productive for all. (4/11/95)

~

President Toda detested formality. For this reason, as his disciple, I have tried to place the foremost emphasis on substance. Formalities are important in certain cases, but mere formality without substance is evil. Formalities in and of themselves have no life; whereas substance lives. Formality is provisional and substance essential. Formality is conventional and therefore conservative, but substance provides the impetus for progress and development. (2/15/90)

~

True joy is to be found in working for kosen-rufu, in practicing and taking action for the happiness of oneself and others. The greatest joy in life is to be found in SGI activities. Our activities for kosen-rufu become memories that shine ever more brilliantly in our lives as time goes by. (7/9/97)

~

True, lasting happiness only and always comes from our own efforts, our own wisdom, our own good fortune. This is a fundamental truth. Faith is the key to strengthening our efforts, our wisdom and good fortune; SGI activities are essential to strengthening ourselves. (3/29/96)

Day in and day out. Today and again tomorrow. Moving of one's own accord to take action, to meet with people and conduct dialogues. This is what Shakyamuni did. Herein lies the correct way of life for human beings and the path of true honor for a Buddhist. This is the rhythm of the SGI's advance — an advance founded upon the same principles espoused and practiced by Shakyamuni and the original Buddha, Nichiren Daishonin. (5/17/95)

This is what I would like to communicate to you, my young friends who are the heirs of the Soka legacy: Live out your lives together with the SGI, an organization fulfilling the Buddha's decree! Our activities in faith constitute our Buddhist practice, lead to the realization of kosen-rufu and enable us to carry out our human revolution. To think selfishly, "I'll just practice on my own and however I like" cannot be called correct faith. Such a person is a Buddhist in name only; he or she is not true a practitioner. (5/5/97)

Spending our time doing what we please may bring momentary pleasure, but it will not bring us true and lasting joy. We cannot become great artists or great actors of life—we cannot become great human beings. Literature, music and drama are all to be found in our activities for faith—in our prayers, in our challenges to develop ourselves through SGI activities and in our efforts to educate others. All value is encompassed in these activities. This is the profound realm of Buddhism. (5/8/98)

I can declare with confidence that each of you who bravely exerts yourself doing Gakkai activities and taking leadership for kosen-rufu, calmly overcoming every obstacle along the way, will enjoy immeasurable benefit. I can state with certitude, too, that each of you is in perfect accord with the Daishonin's spirit. Your efforts win his unrestrained applause and approval. (4/20/98)

As SGI members, our work, our mission, is clear. We have the unparalleled task of working for the happiness of all humanity in an endeavor we call kosen-rufu. To participate in SGI activities and challenge ourselves earnestly on the path of our mission are the greatest sources of happiness. It all comes down to whether we can appreciate this point. (7/16/98)

By devoting ourselves earnestly to SGI activities, we gain the ability to turn difficulties and obstacles into benefit, recognizing that earthly desires and delusions are enlightenment and that the sufferings of birth and death are nirvana. No matter how unpleasant the circumstances we find ourselves in, we can transform them into hope and good fortune—into eternal happiness. How incredible this is! (6/16/98)

DISCUSSION MEETINGS

President Toda said: "You should come home from a discussion meeting feeling happy and inspired from having shared sincere conversation with fellow members—even with only one person, or two. This is the kind of discussion meeting you should strive to hold—even if there is only one person who will listen to what you have to say. Just meeting with that one person is important." (9/18/93)

Making a fresh start toward the goal of SGI-USA becoming the foremost organization in the world, I would like to suggest that "enjoyable meetings and meaningful discussions" be adopted as the new motto for the American organization. (10/2/91)

Every meeting should be lively and cheerful, the type of gathering where everyone leaves feeling: "That was fun. I'm glad I went." (10/2/91)

Significant discussions that foster mutual understanding are much more valuable than the self-complacent pronouncements of one person. Please conduct discussions that deeply penetrate the hearts of the participants—the kind that make them want to say: "That was really refreshing. I have so much hope now. That gave me confidence. I now have the strength to advance." (10/2/91)

In an age of great change, a religion that is dominated by rigid organization or bureaucracy cannot meet the needs of people. For this reason, our discussion meetings and dialogue will henceforth be of increasing importance. As we work to develop and expand the organization, we must pay even greater attention to subtle and minute details. That is, while ensuring that the guiding principles for the organization as a whole are clearly elucidated, we need to focus on fostering the kind of discussion that participants find both convincing and rewarding. These are the two elements necessary for developing a humanistic movement. In this sense, the Soka Gakkai's continuing emphasis on the discussion meeting and new emphasis on holding dialogues place our movement at the forefront of the religious world. (6/10/91)

In any aspect of life, repeating the same thing over and over again may tend to make people weary and bring about stagnation. Therefore, the more important the meeting, the more crucial it becomes to make sure it is always refreshing and meaningful. (1/20/88)

Happiness is found close by. In a world where indifference and inhumanity prevail, let us use our discussion meetings as the pivot for creating oases of peace and harmony in our homes and in our local communities and then extending them to encompass every sphere of society. (3/3/96)

The discussion meetings of the SGI abound in harmony, solidarity and humanism; they represent united gatherings of ordinary people advancing dynamically toward a lofty ideal. This is truly wonderful. (3/3/96)

There is nothing more noble than inviting our friends to discussion meetings, gathering together to enable them to establish a connection with Buddhism, to talk about Buddhist teachings, and to deepen our faith. As the Lotus Sutra clearly indicates, through such steady, dedicated efforts to teach others about Buddhism, you are accumulating the good fortune and benefit to be reborn as great leaders and savor a state of unsurpassed freedom in lifetime after lifetime. (4/23/96)

FIGHTING EVIL

We must ensure that the common people are eternally free from domination by evil tyrants. The people are the base upon which all things rest and the most important factor. A power that does not rely on political authority, that is unswayed by it, is to be found in the power of humanity, of unity and of democracy. We must never allow this power to be diminished. This is the profound significance of the "Buddhism of human revolution," which stimulates and nurtures this human power to the highest degree. (Dialogue 4, 1994)

Only by struggling against the extremes of evil can we live a life of extreme good. That effort will help us create a self that can transcend any obstacle or difficulty with ease and dignity. I hope that all of you, my dear friends in America, will lead lives as champions of justice and happiness. (6/5/96)

Even a tiny speck of evil that causes people to be unhappy should not be tolerated. Attaining "peace and security in this life and good circumstances in the next" exists precisely in carrying out such a struggle with faith and indomitable courage. (LG, p. 243)

President Toda once said: "To really change one's life, to transform it at the very core, one must struggle against great evil. Change cannot be achieved by merely accumulating many small good deeds like so many minute particles of dust. Only in battling against great evil can the mountain of great good, of benefit and fortune, be built." (Dialogue 5, 1994)

Nichiren Daishonin discusses the meaning of the Chinese characters for the word *benefit* (Jpn *kudoku*) as follows: "The *ku* of *kudoku* means to extinguish evil and *doku* means to bring forth good" (*Gosho Zenshu*, p. 762). We fight against those who try to destroy the True Law. That struggle purifies us and brings forth benefit in our lives. Justice or happiness without a battle is just an illusion. Thinking that happiness means a life free of hard work and effort is fantasy. (6/5/96)

Exactly 50 years have passed since Mr. Makiguchi's death in prison. Now is the perfect time for us, as heirs to his noble spirit, to stand up and struggle together with people of conscience throughout the world to protect humanity from the forces of tyranny. (Dialogue 13, 1994)

FRIENDSHIP

There are many different kinds of people in our organization, and each has his or her own mission to fulfill. In this sense, everyone is a child of the Buddha. Therefore, I hope that you will not pass judgment on or exclude anyone based on emotional reasons. Please advance together, chanting for and embracing one another with a magnanimous heart. (2/27/95)

My sincerest wish is that the fundamental relationships among fellow members, our friends and our families will always be bright, joyful and shining with hope. This, of course, also includes members of our families who may not be practicing the Daishonin's Buddhism. The world of faith is held together by warm human bonds forged between caring, cheerful and wise individuals. A cold, bureaucratic organization cannot win the support of many people. (6/4/96)

I hope that the SGI-USA will be pervaded by warm bonds of trust and friendship. An organization that is filled with trust and friendship is strong; it will develop, and its members are happy. Where individuals are on bad terms with one another, there is conflict and suffering. Certainly, such an organization will at some point self-destruct. (2/28/90)

On the journey of kosen-rufu things will not always proceed smoothly. But we are eternal comrades. People who come together in good times but desert one another when the going gets rough are not comrades. Turning a blind eye to the sufferings of others, using the rationale that "it has nothing to do with me" is not the spirit of comrades. True comrades share both sufferings and joy. (LG, p. 245)

Even if someone is close by, their heart may be distant. But if someone is far away, if there is a heart-to-heart bond, they could not be closer. The heart is what counts. In the world of the heart, there is no separation. Chanting daimoku erases distance. (LG, p. 117)

In light of the Gosho, SGI members are precious, noble beings who carry out the work of all Buddhas, bodhisattvas and Buddhist gods. Therefore, let us by all means treasure our fellow members. Let us carry through with faith, filled with gratitude for our profound and mystic connections with one another. (LG, p. 37)

The SGI is a gathering of good friends. It is a world of warm encouragement and shared goals—achieving kosen-rufu, deepening faith and attaining happiness together. That is why it is important that leaders in the SGI be good friends who give their all for the members. Using members for one's own purposes, looking down on them, thinking of them as subordinates at one's beck and call—these are the marks of a bad friend. Such a person will make others lose sight of true faith. I want to make it perfectly clear that there is no need to follow such a leader. (1/20/94)

As the saying goes, it is in times of need that we know our friends. The SGI is a wonderful gathering of good friends. Where else can such a rich world of mutual protection and encouragement—such a golden palace of the people—be found? (LG, p. 36)

Whenever we are suffering from sickness, accidents, natural disasters or some other cause, our fellow members come running straight away to offer encouragement. And when we have cause to rejoice, they join us in celebration. They pray to the Gohonzon with us, are always ready to discuss things, and they join us in taking action. Isn't all this the work of our fellow SGI members? To have such friends is certainly the rarest of good fortune. (LG, p. 36)

Followers reading the Daishonin's letters must have been deeply moved by his warmth. More than a few followers continued to advance with the Daishonin despite great persecutions. That was because of the heart-to-heart bonds that existed between him and each of his followers. It is the same in the SGI. The SGI is strong not because of its organization, but because we create invisible bonds of the heart. (LG, pp. 9–10 ch. 1)

Life is a series of changes, a succession of ups and downs. But those who possess a prime point, a home to which they return no matter what happens, are strong. To come home to the world of friendship in the SGI, to talk things over and prepare for a fresh departure—this is the way I hope all of you will live. When you do, you will advance upon the unerring path to happiness. (6/1/96)

Friendship is strong. Friendship, camaraderie and unity in faith are the heart of the SGI. They come even before the organization. We must never make the mistake of thinking that it is the other way around. The organization serves as a means for deepening friendship, comradeship and faith. To confuse the means with the end is a terrible mistake. (12/16/96)

Those who make many friends have greater opportunities for growth and self-development; they make society a better place and lead happy, satisfying lives. In every situation, human relations—communication and personal interaction—are vital. We need to initiate and nurture friendships and contacts with many people, both within the organization and in society at large. Our lives will open and be enriched to the extent that we do so. (7/9/97)

GAKKAI SPIRIT

Courage is free. Anyone can have it. Courage is another name for the SGI spirit. Mr. Toda said: "The Buddha is filled with compassion, but it is hard for common mortals to show compassion. So we must have courage instead." In other words, when we work courageously for kosen-rufu, our actions by their very nature are compassionate. (5/3/96)

As we advance together with others in the pursuit of our human revolution on the path of unsurpassed joy and self-improvement, we deepen both our wisdom and compassion with the passing of time. This is the SGI way of life. (2/5/93)

Dr. N. Radhakrishnan, director of the Gandhi Smriti and Darshan Samiti (Gandhi Memorial Hall) in New Delhi, has remarked, "The SGI, which is actually struggling against evil today, is a truly Buddhist institution which has inherited the spirit of Shakyamuni." Buddhists who do not fight evil but think only about protecting their own interests are acting against Shakyamuni's spirit. (Dialogue 8, 1994)

To practice just as the Daishonin instructs is the fundamental spirit of the SGI. We are advancing in strict accordance with the Gosho's teachings. As long as we remember this point, we can definitely achieve great victory in life and our efforts for kosen-rufu. (LG, p. 246)

The Daishonin replied from his heart to others' hearts. He replied to sincerity with great sincerity—and with lightning speed. This was also the spirit of Josei Toda, the second Soka Gakkai president. The Soka Gakkai has developed to such an extent because we have maintained their spirits to this day. (LG, p. 9)

President Toda cried out to youth: "In the struggle for the Law in the polluted Latter Day, your desire should be to win the Daishonin's praise as brilliant young warriors. For a person of wisdom, to be praised by fools is the greatest disgrace. To be praised by the great sage is the greatest honor in life." These words, which presidents Makiguchi and Toda both made their motto, are also the Soka Gakkai motto. To put this golden motto into practice is the eternal spirit of the Gakkai. (LG, p. 67)

The people are most important and noble. President Toda was firmly convinced of this point. And I have advanced with the same spirit. This is also Nichiren Daishonin's undying spirit. Please always treasure and protect this organization of the people that is the SGI. (1/6/96)

A coward cannot become a Buddha. We cannot attain Buddhahood unless we possess the heart of a lion. The harsher the situation, the bolder the stand we take. This is the essence of the Soka Gakkai spirit. (7/9/97)

GUIDELINES

(1) Let's value our health first and foremost.

We should never place unreasonable demands on fellow members. To overstrain oneself and to have strong faith are two different things. Unless we are in good health, we cannot fully and unstintingly devote ourselves to activities for kosen-rufu.

We should advance with wisdom and common sense, and show actual proof through our good health and longevity.

(2) Let's relate our experiences.

One fact is more powerful than a million theoretical arguments. By promoting a movement to share our personal experiences in faith with others, let us spread the joy of faith in and understanding about Buddhism in our local communities, in society and throughout the United States.

(3) Let's encourage others by phone.

It is important to use our wisdom. America is such a vast country that the telephone serves as a valuable way to keep in contact with and give encouragement to members with whom distance makes it difficult to meet regularly. As stated in the Gosho, "The voice does the Buddha's work" (*Gosho Zenshu,* p. 708). Your warm and friendly voices on the phone will greatly encourage your members.

(4) Let's promote a "no accidents" campaign.

Traffic accidents, in particular, bring suffering and sadness not only to those who are involved but also to their friends and loved ones. Through strong prayers, we should strive to lead each day without any kind of accident.

(5) Let's engage in joyful dialogue and hold happy discussion meetings.

There is no need for us to be hasty or impatient in our efforts for kosen-rufu. Through our continuous and earnest devotion to such fundamentals as gongyo, personal guidance and discussion meetings, we will be able to scale the mountain of attaining enlightenment and realize kosen-rufu. Also, as we continue to engage in joyful, heart-to-heart dialogue with one another and conduct happy, cheerful discussion meetings, we will surely come to accumulate enduring good fortune in our own lives. (9/19/93)

JUSTICE

I hope that you will always speak the truth boldly, saying what needs to be said no matter whom you're addressing. When it comes to championing a just cause, you must never be cowardly, never fawn, never try to curry favor. (4/20/98)

I hope that people of faith will live with the spirit of "uncrowned kings and queens," depending neither on power and authority nor on mere wealth. I think it was Shakespeare who said that a heart with the spirit of justice is like wearing a triple-coat of armor, whereas a heart that is corrupt is like being naked even when girthed in steel. (Dialogue 2, 1994)

There is a saying that "Speech is silver, silence is golden." But when you are engaged in a struggle, the opposite is true. Then, speaking out is golden and silence is defeat. It is vital that we speak out, that we boldly declare what is true and what is false. Unfounded criticisms must be rebutted and the record set straight. (Dialogue 4, 1994)

What matters most is that we fight thoroughly against injustice with a lofty, dauntless spirit. While waging a determined struggle against evil that nearly cost him his life, Nichiren Daishonin cried out [to Shijo Kingo, as they were being led to the execution grounds at Tatsunokuchi], "You should be delighted at this great fortune" (MW-1, 181). And he wholeheartedly anticipated that his disciples would "form their ranks and follow him" (MW-1, 176). (LG, p. 243)

Justice is like the sun. A society that lacks justice is shrouded in darkness. No one can stop the sun from rising. No cloud can hide the rays of the sun indefinitely. "Opening the eyes" means causing those hearts steeped in darkness to recognize the rising sun of justice. (LG, p. 59)

We have to make ourselves heard. We have to speak out for what we believe. When we, the people, boldly state our true convictions—never losing our optimism or sense of humor—the times will change. When it comes to speaking out for justice, there isn't any need for restraint. On the contrary, to be reserved or hesitant under such circumstances is wrong. (9/25/97)

The powerful may appear great, but in reality they are not. Greatest of all are ordinary people. If those in power lead lives of idle luxury it is because the people are silent. We have to speak out. With impassioned words, we need to resolutely attack abuses of power that cause people suffering. This is fighting for justice. It is wrong to remain silent when confronted with injustice. Doing so is tantamount to supporting and condoning evil. (5/8/98)

KOSEN-RUFU

The Soka Gakkai's goal is kosen-rufu—realizing human happiness and world peace by widely spreading the philosophy and ideals of Nichiren Daishonin's Buddhism. We will continue to strive earnestly for this goal, undaunted by criticism, slander or malicious attempts to hinder our progress. Because what we are doing is the will and decree of the original Buddha, Nichiren Daishonin, I proclaim that all who energetically exert themselves for the cause of kosen-rufu are genuine disciples of the Daishonin, genuine members of the SGI. (4/20/98)

~

A Buddha holds others in the highest regard; the ability to do so is the Buddha's intrinsic virtue. Kosen-rufu means promulgating this attitude of respect for human beings. (LG, p. 44)

~

To triumph in life and to achieve kosen-rufu, there is no strategy superior to the Lotus Sutra (Nam-myoho-renge-kyo). Nichiren Daishonin urges, "Employ the strategy of the Lotus Sutra before any other" (MW-1, 246). In other words, we must first pray with an earnest and determined commitment to conquer negative forces, then continue praying. We need to display wholehearted wisdom, ingenuity, action and unity. (Dialogue 3, 1994)

~

Joy is not simply your personal, egoistic happiness. Nor is it making others happy at the expense of your own happiness. You and others delighting together, you and others becoming happy together—this is the Mystic Law and the wondrous thing about our realm of kosen-rufu. The Daishonin states, "Joy means that both oneself and others have wisdom and compassion" (*Gosho Zenshu,* p. 761). (2/5/93)

~

From the outset, America has been a country to which people from around the world have flocked, leaving their homelands for one reason or another. They have come to this country searching for a new home. It is the task of the kosen-rufu movement to breathe life into America's purpose, building a new home for these people. Society will become a genuine home to all only when it provides each person with absolute peace and compassionate protection. (2/25/90)

∼

Various misunderstandings or resistance may be met with in any country. But such is the destiny of those who introduce something new. It is by overcoming those negative forces, replacing old maps with new ones, that the movement for kosen-rufu will be carried forth. (2/26/90)

∼

Our spirit changes our being. It changes our lives. Why does the Buddha have an indestructible, diamond-like life? Shakyamuni explains it is because he has steadfastly and thoroughly protected the True Law. Having a strong spirit for kosen-rufu enables us to develop diamond-like lives. (LG, p. 135)

∼

A small fire can easily be extinguished by a gust of wind. But with a large fire, it is just the opposite—the stronger the wind, the higher and more furiously it blazes. Great difficulties are a tailwind for the advance of kosen-rufu. (LG, p. 125)

∼

Those who struggle to the full extent of their abilities now, at this time, will also gain eternal honor. Imagine 100 or 200 years hence when our descendants proudly say, "Think of it, my ancestors devoted their lives to kosen-rufu in this area." (LG, p. 113)

∼

Please hold your heads high, thoroughly dedicating yourselves to the great goal of kosen-rufu, regardless of what may arise, always chanting daimoku with clear and resonant voices. In doing so, you are paving the way for a journey throughout the three existences, endowed with the four noble qualities of eternity, happiness, true self and purity. This is a state of life in which you can experience both life and death with great joy. (1/30/93)

The important thing is to keep working for kosen-rufu to the very end. On any journey, we cannot hope to reach our destination if we stop halfway. Likewise, if despite our good fortune in meeting and embarking on the unsurpassed way of Buddhism, we stop halfway, all the efforts we have made thus far will have been in vain; we will not be able to attain Buddhahood. (5/23/96)

The greater our efforts to advance kosen-rufu, the greater the benefit and eternal good fortune we accumulate in our lives. The more outstanding people we foster, the stronger and healthier we become. The more aware we are of our responsibility, the more joy we experience. Such are the workings of the Buddhist Law. (3/20/96)

Kosen-rufu is a supreme, golden path extending throughout the Latter Day of the Law into the eternal future. Let us continue to advance boldly and intrepidly along this path as Nichiren Daishonin teaches. This is the way world peace will be accomplished. If we do not widely spread the principles and ideals of the Daishonin's Buddhism, there will be no hope for the peace and happiness of humankind. (4/21/98)

We are no longer in an age when one person can shoulder everything. Of course, for the day-to-day running of the organization, someone will still be officially designated as president, but ultimately, our future development hinges on every member having the commitment required of a Soka Gakkai president. With this spirit, this sense of responsibility, this leadership in your activities, may you always work for kosen-rufu and for the victory of the people. May you also build a Soka Gakkai where everyone can advance joyfully—a Soka Gakkai of undying progress. (3/13/98)

MENTOR AND DISCIPLE

The lifeblood of Buddhism exists only in the correct faith actually manifested in people's lives. Correct faith—the vehicle of the lifeblood of Buddhism—is transmitted through the mentor and disciple relationship. Only when we follow the teachings of Nichiren Daishonin and Nikko Shonin can we perpetuate the pure flow of the Daishonin's Buddhism for eternity. Should we follow the corrupt stream of Niko, who betrayed his master's teachings, we would commit the serious offense of destroying the heart of Buddhism. (10/1/91)

When the Daishonin is no longer in the world, it is his writings—the Gosho—that we should make our master. So long as we continue practicing in accordance with the Gosho, what possible confusion can there be? (10/1/91)

One must not simply allow evil teachers who go against the master to carry on their ways—this is the fundamental spirit of Nikko Shonin. It is the spirit with which he abandoned Mount Minobu, where the pure flow of faith had become polluted due to the actions of Hakiri Sanenaga, who was misled by the evil teacher Niko. (9/30/91)

"If one should forget the original teacher who brought him the water of wisdom from the great ocean of the Lotus Sutra and instead follow another, he is sure to sink into the endless sufferings of life and death" (MW-1, 164). Thus the Daishonin strictly admonishes us. To follow the Daishonin who is the "original teacher" is the very meaning of our faith. (9/30/91)

I am determined to work still harder to draw attention to the greatness of the ideals and philosophy of presidents Makiguchi and Toda. I fear not persecution or schemes. I am the son of a lion, a disciple of Mr. Toda. I hope that the members of the youth division, as my young successors, will embrace this Soka Gakkai spirit as their own and carry on in my footsteps. (2/24/96)

When Mr. Toda was released from prison, the Soka Gakkai was left with only a handful of members. Even before the war, the membership had stood at only about 3,000. The organization's presence in Japanese society was, therefore, minuscule. Nevertheless, Mr. Toda characterized President Makiguchi as "a great man of global stature." And he encouraged us to be aware that we are disciples of this outstanding individual. Nobility is the mark of a true disciple. And Mr. Toda was an example of an exceptional disciple. (2/24/96)

Once a path is opened, those who follow can travel with composure and ease. Nichiren Daishonin, as the Buddha of the Latter Day, possessing the virtues of sovereign, teacher and parent, opened a path to enlightenment for all people. For this we owe him our eternal gratitude. To extend and expand the path that the mentor has graciously opened is the disciples' mission. (LG, p. 64)

~

Ultimately, Buddhism comes down to the person. I did not wait to place my trust in President Toda until after I had learned about the Daishonin's teachings. Rather, I came to trust Buddhism because I first believed in the person, Josei Toda. (LG, p. 34)

~

The Daishonin says, "If Nichiren had not appeared, the Buddha's words would have withered." The spirit to not allow the words of the original Buddha, Nichiren Daishonin, to have been in vain is the fundamental spirit of the Soka Gakkai. This was the spirit of Tsunesaburo Makiguchi, and of Josei Toda. This is the spirit of a disciple. (LG, p. 19)

~

Mr. Toda felt deep appreciation toward his mentor, President Makiguchi, to whom in a memorial he would later say, "In your vast and boundless compassion, you allowed me to come with you even to prison." This eloquently sums up their solemn, magnificent relationship as mentor and disciple. (LG, p. 15)

~

President Makiguchi's disciple and successor, Josei Toda, was also jailed, confined to a solitary cell. Mr. Toda then embarked on a solemn quest to master the essence of the Lotus Sutra. No doubt he celebrated his mentor's birthday in solitude as he continued to plumb the depths of the law of life, striving to find a way to human revolution. He was fast approaching the profound insight and enlightenment that he attained in his prison cell that would serve as a fundamental means of spiritual liberation for humanity. We of the SGI are proudly following in the footsteps of these two great champions of peace, human rights and freedom. (1/30/93)

It should be pointed out that the "Law," not the "person," is to be regarded as the proper standard in all things. Putting the person first gives you an uncertain standard; it is to let that person's mind become your master. In contrast, if you establish the Law as your standard, you will become the master of your mind. (2/21/90)

I hope you members of the youth division will, in the spirit of Shijo Kingo, advance with the Daishonin and also with Mr. Makiguchi, Mr. Toda and myself. This spirit of joint struggle shared by mentor and disciple is the very heart of the SGI. It represents a solidarity in which people are linked by true unity of purpose and commitment. May each one of you lead the most valuable, meaningful youth. The age belongs to you. (5/3/96)

True character is forged only through hardship and suffering. Moreover, it is the mentor–disciple relationship, not organizational structure, that builds character. Many great scholars, pioneers and leaders of the world have come to know how crucial the mentor–disciple relationship is. (7/19/96)

As direct disciples of the Daishonin, we have summoned forth the three powerful enemies of Buddhism. Defeating their schemes and repelling their onslaughts, we have carved out a great path of kosen-rufu. This has been the unrivaled pride of Mr. Makiguchi, Mr. Toda and myself as Soka Gakkai presidents. It is indisputable proof that the Soka Gakkai is the foremost organization in the entire world acting in accord with the Buddha's will and decree. (4/20/98)

Those who have a mentor in life are truly fortunate. The path of mentor and disciple is one that leads to personal development and growth. Those without a mentor may appear free and unbeholden to anyone, but without a solid standard or model on which to base themselves, their lives become aimless and wandering. (5/23/96)

ORGANIZATION

President Toda said: "Those who do not value the organization are practicing self-centered faith. With such faith you cannot expect to receive the truly profound benefits of this practice." Working hard within the organization for people's happiness and welfare is itself the truly noble Buddhist practice. (5/26/97)

There is no need to be impatient. Anything that is accomplished quickly and easily will not long endure. Now is the time to concentrate on the construction of a solid foundation. I hope you will complete this work slowly but surely, filled with hope and joy. (2/13/90)

Those who advance together with this organization that is dedicated to kosen-rufu and pervaded by benefit will evolve the correct mind of faith that matches the time. With this mind of faith you can fill the canvas of your lives with portraits of happiness in which all your wishes are fulfilled. (1/31/93)

~

Schooling, career, social status and the like are not the goal. The people are most important and most noble. President Toda was firmly convinced of this point. And I have advanced with the same spirit. This is also Nichiren Daishonin's undying spirit. Please always treasure and protect this organization of the people that is the SGI. (1/6/96)

~

President Toda once described the Soka Gakkai as "the kosen-rufu organization which is more precious to me than my life." There were arrogant priests who denigrated Mr. Toda's statement, scornfully saying, "Life is more precious by far." Having no thought whatsoever of trying to accomplish kosen-rufu themselves, they could not possibly have understood his spirit. (3/3/96)

~

Absolute conviction and passion toward faith—not leadership positions or orders—are the organization's driving force. People who have lost the pure passion of faith must not be allowed to exploit the organization. Taking advantage of faith or using the organization for unpure purposes cannot be tolerated. (3/3/96)

~

In the harsh reality of society, competition and tension cannot be avoided. You may also sometimes experience clashes of ego. But once you return to the home of the SGI-USA, you can let go of your tension, relax and smile. This is where

you can obtain "nutrition" for your life, thereby feeling refreshed and filled with energy to undertake the next day's
challenge. As leaders, it is your duty to make the SGI-USA
such an organization. (2/25/90)

Buddhism exists for the sake of each person's happiness. The
same can be said of the SGI movement for kosen-rufu. The
organization exists for the sake of the people, not the other
way around. To embrace and protect all individuals, leading
them to happiness and attaining Buddhahood—this is why
the SGI-USA exists. (2/25/90)

I would like you to build an enviable, endearing SGI-USA
family, of which those around you will say: "Those people
seem truly happy. How warm the light from the window of
that SGI-USA house looks!" Steadily infusing society with
smiling faces and hope, please construct, with the Mystic Law
as your foundation, an eternal family of peace and a happy
and beautiful America. (2/25/90)

In the organization, we have to clearly say what must be said.
The purpose of Buddhism is not to produce dupes who
blindly follow their leader. It is to produce people of wisdom
who can judge right or wrong on their own in the clear mirror of Buddhism. (2/27/90)

In a buffalo herd, all the individuals in the group follow the
lead buffalo; they go where he wants to go and they do what
he wants to do. In other words, they merely wait for the in-
structions of the leader. When human organizations follow
this model, they also become an unthinking herd. Unable to

adapt to changing times, such organizations travel a course to inevitable decline. (6/23/96)

In a successful organization, some authors propose using a model based on the image of a flock of geese. The flock of geese that they envisage is flying in a "V" formation, with the leadership of the flock changing frequently as different geese take turns leading the way. It is a model in which everyone in the organization takes responsibility, everyone is equal and everyone unites together solidly in their shared objective. An organization of this kind, the authors argue, will be successful in the changing times in which we live. (6/23/96)

You should put energy into the development of the women's division. An organization where the women's division can freely conduct activities, where its opinions are respected, is healthy and strong. Such an organization can make steady progress and will seldom spin its wheels. (2/21/90)

If I were to make an analogy, thought and philosophy would be the heart or respiratory system of the human body. When the heart is sound, the whole body can maintain healthy activity. This same principle applies to the individual and society. The SGI has a mission to serve as the heart that ensures the healthy functioning of society. Consequently, taking good care of the SGI (the heart) allows the fresh life-giving blood of humanism to flow to and nourish all areas of society, including culture, politics and the economy. (1/28/93)

There may be times, certainly, when being a member of an organization seems bothersome and we just want to be alone.

But how sad it is if we are left alone without any support and then lose faith. True growth comes from striving together with fellow members in the living realm of human beings, experiencing the rich gamut of human emotion. (12/16/96)

I would like each of you to rise to the challenge of revolutionizing the area where you live into an ideal community and to do so with the determination to start from where you are right now. This means building a good SGI organization in your local area—and building it yourself with loving, painstaking care, the way an artist pours his or her heart and soul into creating a work of art. It also means fostering capable people. Buddhism, after all, can only flourish if there are people who uphold and practice its teachings. (8/27/97)

The organization of faith is not something that holds you back or restricts you. Rather, it is a springboard that enables you to develop yourself to the utmost and to lead the most dynamic existence. It is the most precious place for carrying out our Buddhist practice. (5/5/97)

PERSECUTION

At present, only we of the SGI are encountering great persecution for the sake of kosen-rufu, and in doing so, we read the Gosho with our lives. We are the only ones forging ahead along this honorable path in strict accordance with the Lotus Sutra and the Gosho. This is proof that the SGI is an organization committed to carrying out the Buddha's decree. (2/24/96)

Viewed from the perspective of the Buddhist principle of cause and effect, those who harass and torment the children of the Buddha are destined to meet with great suffering themselves. The law of cause and effect is strict and uncompromising. On the other hand, those who praise the children of the Buddha will be able to construct a life of great and enduring good fortune as lofty and indomitable as the Himalayan peaks. (6/23/96)

~

Emerson writes: "Without enemies, no hero. The sun were insipid, if the universe were not opaque." In other words, because there are enemies, people can become heroes. Because there is darkness, the sun, illuminating darkness, is great. (1/6/96)

~

When neighbors say nasty things [about this Buddhism and its practitioners], that's an example of the first of the three powerful enemies—lay people ignorant of Buddhism. When priests defame the Law and its practitioners, that's an example of the second—arrogant and cunning priests. And when a person who is looked up to by society as a great leader joins forces with the authorities and persecutes the practitioners of the Lotus Sutra, that's an example of the third—false saints. (Dialogue 5, 1994)

~

Mr. Toda once said: "I will tell you when we can accomplish kosen-rufu. It will happen when the three powerful enemies make their appearance. The time will be especially ripe for kosen-rufu when the third group—false saints—appear. They are the most frightening of the three enemies. Yet I shall rejoice when they appear. I would like you all to feel the same

way. When that time comes, let us fight with all our might."
(Dialogue 4, 1994)

Encountering great persecution for the sake of Buddhism is
actually an event for rejoicing. All too often, however, people
tend to shun, fear or turn tail when they see alarming obstacles heading their way. If we do so, we cannot attain Buddhahood. (3/3/96)

For a Buddhist, persecution is the supreme honor. The SGI is
the true heir of Nichiren Daishonin's teachings. We always act
in strict accordance with the Gosho and the teachings of the
Lotus Sutra, advancing with unwavering confidence. That is
why we face persecutions. I know that the Daishonin is praising us with all his heart. (2/5/96)

The Daishonin says, "One who perseveres through great persecution and embraces the sutra from beginning to end is the
Buddha's emissary" (MW-3, 290). At times of great persecution, we must summon forth strong faith, chant resolute
daimoku and speak out for justice. We have to offer prayers
with the spirit to squarely face the persecution and struggle
selflessly. Those who do so will become Buddhas. (LG, p. 228)

Unless people possess firm conviction in their hearts—unless
they can honestly say to themselves, "I will never compromise
on this point" and "I will stake my life on defending this ideal"—they will be swayed, unable to resist the pressures of the
majority. Of course, it will then be even more difficult for

them to endure persecution at the hands of the authorities. (LG, p. 223)

The Daishonin was an exile, completely without freedom. He was confined to the tiny island of Sado, a natural prison. President Toda once said, "In modern terms, exile to Sado is comparable to being banished to the Sahara Desert." Yet the Daishonin's spirit was that of a king. No one could bind his heart in chains. No sword of persecution could make the slightest nick in his armored spirit. (LG, p. 70)

Mr. Makiguchi did not regard it as shameful to undergo criticism or persecution for the sake of the Lotus Sutra. He died in prison for his beliefs because he propagated Nam-myoho-renge-kyo of the Three Great Secret Laws, the essence of the Lotus Sutra, based on the conviction that to be praised by fools is the greatest disgrace and to be praised by the great sage [Nichiren Daishonin] is the greatest glory. I believe that he provides the foremost model for all who embrace faith in the Buddhism of Nichiren Daishonin. (LG, p. 67)

To prove the proposition "Buddhism is true," the Daishonin deliberately drew out negative forces and challenged them. Without such a great struggle, even the most outstanding scripture would, in the end, be no more than a book. Even the most profound sutra would be mere words. The sutra's words only become Buddhism, only become a genuine religion, when they are put to the test in life. (LG, p. 18)

"During these more than twenty years, I have never known even an hour or a moment of peace," the Daishonin says. He lived this way for us. How merciful! His was a great struggle for spiritual revolution more intense than any battle. From the time the Daishonin established his teaching at age 32, great persecutions rained down upon him. Still, he never retreated a single step. (LG, p. 13)

The Daishonin took tremendous pride in having undergone great persecution. In this, we can sense the heart of the indomitable lion king. We are the Daishonin's disciples. We carry on his great struggle. This is the greatest possible honor. Compared with the great persecutions the Daishonin underwent, to be called a few names hardly amounts to anything. (LG, p. 246)

Unless we construct a life of such depth and profundity that we will go to prison willingly and cheerfully for the sake of our convictions, we cannot be called a genuine leader. We must be willing to live out our lives by regarding persecution as an honor. (4/2/95)

RELIGIOUS REFORMATION

The great American poet and philosopher Ralph Waldo Emerson (1803–82), who had close ties to Boston, wrote in his diary (in 1872):"One thing is certain: the religions are obsolete when the reforms do not proceed from them."The energy to bring about fresh and vibrant reform exists within a living religion. A living religion constantly routs out apathy and force of habit and stirs up a fresh, new breeze. (9/18/93)

Without common sense, religion develops into blind belief and fanaticism, which have no place in Buddhism. The Daishonin writes: "Buddhism is reason. Reason will win over your lord" (MW-3, 238). In other words, reason will win over authority. (9/30/91)

The history of the Soka Gakkai has been a continuous battle against authoritarianism, which hinders human growth. In its course, we have taken our movement promoting true democracy to all parts of the world. For this, we have been the target of constant criticism and persecution. Therefore, we must have keen perception to see through devilish functions and continue to wage battle against evil without retreating an inch. This is the way we can protect the True Law, faith, the Buddha's children and democracy. (9/23/91)

The Buddhism of Nichiren Daishonin is the law that enables all people, wherever they may be, to carry out the highest practice of faith and gain the supreme benefit of attaining Buddhahood. It is the teaching that enables each person to cultivate the greatest wisdom, lead the most respectworthy life and attain the greatest happiness. Authoritarianism has no place in this Buddhism, nor does the "demonization of religion," which turns a teaching into a lever for oppressing the people. (9/29/91)

The original teaching of Buddhism is that our actions during our lifetimes are what fundamentally determine our fates after death. There are, of course, memorial services for the deceased in Buddhism. But here again, it is sincere prayers made by a person who upholds faith in the True Law that are communicated and extend benefits to the life-entity of the deceased. It is not the ceremony itself that is important. It is sending waves of love and good wishes from the heart of one who believes in the Mystic Law to the heart of another that is important. (Dialogue 2, 1994)

President Makiguchi vehemently denounced the Japanese clergy who collaborated with militarist authorities during World War II, declaring, "We must make a frontal assault on this enemy!" President Toda also left us the admonition, "You must never let up in your struggle against evil." Let us apply ourselves to this grand spiritual struggle with ever greater vigor so that we may usher in an era of the common people in the twenty-first century. (1/30/93)

The purpose of faith is certainly not to subjugate oneself to the authority of temples or clergy but, as my mentor clearly stated, to enable every person to attain a happiness that endures eternally throughout the three existences of life. (1/27/93)

It is plain that the members of the Nichiren Shoshu priesthood today, in their decadent conduct, are the exact opposite of the Daishonin. The opposite of the Buddha is the devil, the enemy of the Buddha. Nichiren Daishonin could not possibly condone the priesthood today, which has trampled on the sincere hard-earned offerings people have made. (LG, p. 33)

Mr. Makiguchi said to Mr. Toda these famous words: "What I deplore is not merely the ruin of a single school, but the fact that the entire country is sliding toward destruction.... Isn't it time to remonstrate with the government? What on earth is

the priesthood afraid of? What's your opinion, Mr. Toda?"
These words, arising as they do from courage, compassion
and spiritual freedom, indicate the true meaning of tolerance.
One month later, both Mr. Makiguchi and Mr. Toda were ar-
rested. (Dialogue 13, 1994)

There are those, like the members of the Nichiren Shoshu
priesthood today, who are under the illusion that they are absolute, who arrogantly suppose themselves different from and
better than others. In light of the Gosho, such people definitely are not practicing the Daishonin's Buddhism.
(LG, p. 40)

TWENTY-FIRST CENTURY

From now until the year 2005, let us all take good care of our
health and live out our lives. Let us also work to further secure, for all eternity, the future of the SGI—a precious jewel
to which no other compares in the universe. And as an organization which "knows neither old age or death," let us devote ourselves to building an even more solid foundation for
cultivating talented individuals. (3/9/96)

A Kenyan saying goes that we should treat the earth well; it is
not a gift from our parents but a loan from our children. But
the adults of our day are leaving a dismal inheritance to today's young people and the children you may have. It is your
legacy, so you must act. You who have not forgotten the beauty and wonder of the earth must speak out. Your struggle to
protect the twenty-first century, your century, the century of
life, has already begun. (DOY 2, ch. 17)

The twentieth century was a century of war and peace, a century of politics and economics. The dawning twenty-first century holds the promise, however, of a century of humanity and culture, a century of both science and religion. I hope all of you will advance on this wonderful new path of humanism with pride and confidence, as gallant philosophers of action. (4/2/98)

There is no place in the SGI for cowards or for egoists who are prone to arbitrary or self-serving views. Our movement has no need for the fainthearted, filled with doubt, who readily succumb to negative influences. Let us strive for the Law and live with dignity as proud members of the SGI! The twenty-first century shall be the essential phase of our movement. Bathed in the brilliant light of dawn, let us take our places on that golden stage. Let us lead truly magnificent lives! (4/21/98)

UNITY

In "The True Entity of Life," it says: "If you are of the same mind as Nichiren, you must be a Bodhisattva of the Earth. And since you are a Bodhisattva of the Earth, there is not the slightest doubt that you have been a disciple of the Buddha from the remotest past" (MW-1, 93). From Mr. Makiguchi's time, the Soka Gakkai has always been an organization whose members are all "of the same mind as Nichiren." (2/5/96)

In a family, if one person is unhappy, then so is the entire family. Therefore, I would like you to sincerely pray for and protect one another so that there are no people who are unfortunate and unhappy, or who abandon their faith, and that every person will become happy. These are the kinds of humanistic bonds among fellow members that give birth to true unity. Coercion or force stemming from power and authority is ineffective at critical moments. (2/25/90)

No one can regulate religious beliefs or our activities based on faith. I hope you will always live in unity with the original Buddha, pursuing faith as disciples who are "of the same mind as Nichiren." Unfazed by the petty jealousies of others, please move forward boldly, with joy and laughter. (2/5/96)

[In the term "disrupting the unity of the Buddhist order," one of the five cardinal sins,] "Buddhist order" (Skt. *samgha*) does not refer only to priests [but also to the laity]. Since we in the Soka Gakkai are faithfully practicing Nichiren Daishonin's teachings and striving in harmonious unity to realize kosen-rufu, anyone who attempts to destroy our organization is certain to suffer greatly. (3/8/96)

Always live as harmonious family members of the Mystic Law, embodying the spirit of many in body, one in mind. No matter what happens, I hope that you will continue to advance, directing your hearts toward unity and friendship. (2/28/90)

We suffer together, rejoice together and bring our lives to fruition together. We regard both suffering and joy as facts of life, chanting Nam-myoho-renge-kyo no matter what happens. To maintain this comradeship, this single-minded commitment to faith, is our eternal guideline in advancing toward kosen-rufu. Let us ever advance with strong unity in faith! (LG, p. 245)

There are many differences, for instance, in age or position, between human beings. The question is how can we use these differences to create perfect harmony? We have to realize that besides creating harmony, we can, given the opportunity, make a complicated and emotionally entangled world. Whether we make our organization harmonious or disunited depends on each person's *ichinen* or mind. In other words, each member having a seeking mind to learn from other people is crucial. In this sense, as the Daishonin teaches, we learn from one another, respect one another, protect one another, and thus live humbly for the Law and for kosen-rufu with the Gohonzon as our basis. (6/21/88)

It was not authority that united the Daishonin and his followers; nor was it their concern for profit. They were united in heart. For this reason, their bond was indestructible. For this reason, their lives overflowed with benefit and their connection was lofty and eternal. (LG, p. 119)

When we base ourselves on the spirit of "one in mind," there is neither envy nor backbiting. Nor is there shirking of responsibility. Instead, we can manifest strong, broad-minded faith, and our lives will overflow with benefit. Josei Toda said time and again, "Unity is the basis of guidance for the Soka Gakkai." (LG, p. 97)

The new vitality of American society is produced by returning to the starting point—to the ideals on which your country was founded. Similarly, you should also reconfirm the fundamental path of faith, practice and study and make a fresh departure based on the unity of many in body, one in mind—the starting point of our movement. This is the key to the reconstruction of the SGI–USA as a model organization. (2/21/90)

Peace, Culture and Education

ART

If you allow yourself to be swayed by the opinions of others — "It must be good, because everyone else likes it" "It must be bad, because no one else likes it"—your feelings, your sensibility, which should be the very core of artistic experience, will wither and die. To enjoy art to the fullest, you must abandon preconceived notions, leaving a blank slate. Then confront the work directly with your entire being. If you are deeply moved, then that work is, for you, a great work of art. (DOY 2, ch. 16)

A great work of art is one that truly moves and inspires you. You yourself must be moved. Don't look at art with others' eyes. Don't listen to music with others' ears. You must react to art with your own feelings, your own heart and mind. (DOY 2, ch. 16)

The renowned French sculptor Auguste Rodin (1840–1917) said that the important thing for artists is to feel, to love, to hope, to tremble, to live. It is to be, before an artist, he said, a human being. The human feelings of hope, love, anger and fear are communicated to us through the artist's work. The vibrations of the artist's spirit set off similar vibrations within our hearts. It is a shared feeling that links the creator and the viewer, transcending the boundaries of time and space. (DOY 2, ch. 15)

Art is the cry of the soul from the core of one's being. Creating and appreciating art set free the joyous soul trapped deep within us. That is why art causes such joy. Art, quite aside from any question of skill or its lack, is the emotion, the pleasure of expressing one's life exactly as it is. Those who see such art are moved by its passion, its strength, its intensity and its beauty. That is why it is impossible to separate fully human life from art. (DOY 2, ch. 16)

The institutions of human society treat us as parts of a machine. They assign us ranks and place considerable pressure upon us to fulfill defined roles. We need something to help us restore our lost and distorted humanity. Each of us has feelings that have been suppressed and have built up inside. There is a voiceless cry resting in the depths of our souls, waiting for expression. Art gives the soul's feelings voice and form. (DOY 2, ch. 16)

Life is painful. It has thorns, like the stem of a rose. Culture and art are the roses that bloom on the stem. The flower is yourself, your humanity. Art is the liberation of the humanity inside yourself. (DOY 2, ch. 16)

We have to live. We work, we eat our daily bread and we grow old. Our lives are a constant repetition of little deeds. Against that backdrop, we progress, we seek a more fully human existence, we desire to make a flower bloom. From that feeling, culture and art are born. (DOY 2, ch. 16)

People who appreciate art and culture are important. Cultured people value peace and lead others to a world of beauty, hope and bright tomorrows. Tyrannical authority, on the other hand, only leads people to darkness—the opposite of art. For that reason, nurturing and spreading an appreciation for art and culture are crucial to creating peace. (DOY 2, ch. 15)

In the arts, as in other fields, the words of people of true greatness mirror the teachings of Buddhism. This is because, at the very core of their beings, such people are striving ever to direct themselves toward the fundamental law of the universe. (2/24/96)

BUDDHISM IN SOCIETY

Today's world is sorely lacking hope, a positive vision for the future and a solid philosophy. There is no bright light illuminating the horizon. That is precisely why we, the Bodhisattvas of the Earth, have appeared. That is why Nichiren Daishonin's Buddhism of the sun is essential. We stand up, holding high the torch of courage in one hand and the philosophy of truth and justice in the other. We have begun to take action to break boldly through the darkness of the four sufferings of birth, old age, sickness and death, as well as the darkness in society and the world. (6/19/96)

Buddhism is found in the realities of society and daily life. Because Buddhism is in no way separate from these realities, we must strive through our actions and behavior to be exemplary models for others. (4/13/96)

Buddhism teaches that one characteristic of a bodhisattva is perceiving the world's sounds. The insight needed to correctly discern and grasp developments in society and the times— even to anticipate them before they happen—is indispensable. (4/2/98)

Today, we live in an age where opportunities for profound life-to-life inspiration are all but nonexistent. Idle amusements bring only fleeting pleasure. They produce neither profound inspiration nor growth for one's life. In contrast, Buddhism exists to enable people to realize personal growth and to improve their lives. Buddhism is always rooted in the reality of life. It is the wellspring of wisdom for bringing harmony and happiness to our families, communities and society at large. (3/3/96)

Broadly speaking, creating a land of peace and tranquillity — as in the passage, "This, my land, remains safe and tranquil"— indicates the virtue of the sovereign. Education represents the virtue of the teacher. And culture, because it fosters people's inner lives, relates to the virtue of the parent. We are extending this path of the three virtues throughout the entire world. (LG, p. 64)

Human society, viewed with the eye of Buddhism, takes on a completely different meaning as discerned by secular eyes.

No longer are the powerful above and ordinary people below. Status does not make people great, and authority does
not make them noble. Instead, it is people wholeheartedly
dedicated to a lofty ideal who shine the brightest. (LG, p. 137)

There are various careers and roles that people fill in society.
While each role, of course, is significant, the fundamental role
that we play as Buddhists is that of philosophers of life and of
humanity who can impart eternal value to humankind. We
are leaders of happiness and creators of peace. In this sense,
our role is unique. (2/25/90)

The principle that "Buddhism equals life" means that everything in one's life is itself Buddhism. The principle that "Buddhism becomes manifest in society" means that society, too, is
at one with Buddhism. The struggle for kosen-rufu can be
waged only within the realities of life and society. Those who
earnestly grapple with these realities develop strength and inner substance. They develop and grow. (10/25/96)

COMMON SENSE

Buddhism is reason. It doesn't exist apart from society or
apart from reality. That is why it is important for each of us
to cultivate good judgment and common sense. We must respect and harmonize with society's ways. Respecting the life
of each individual, we work among the people. This is the
SGI's fundamental creed. (4/19/97)

Buddhism is reason. It is vital therefore, that our lives and our
activities in society accord with reason. Please manifest the

principle of "faith equals daily life" so that you will be trusted, respected and emulated by others. Bringing fragrant flowers of trust and humanism to bloom throughout society is one of the goals of Buddhism. To do things that others find strange and unnatural, that run counter to common sense—these actions go against the basic tenets of Buddhism and amount to slander of the Law. (4/13/96)

CREATIVITY

If we only repeat what we have seen and heard, we will never advance beyond imitation. The mind is crucial. We have to experience with the mind and express with the mind to be innovative. That requires blood, sweat and tears; it requires relentless searching and personal effort. Only then do we gradually acquire the ability to express ourselves fully and naturally. (DOY 2, ch. 16)

Being creative is very different than being self-centered, just as genuine individuality and an invented, eccentric persona differ. In fact, it may well be that truly unique individuals express their uniqueness without even trying. They seek and accept nature, life and truth and convey them exactly as they are. In the process, their individuality naturally shines through. This is true creativity, true innovation. I think the French sculptor Auguste Rodin (1840–1917) meant the same thing when he said that life is more important than individuality in the creation of art. (DOY 2, ch. 16)

Creativity is a fierce struggle. Creative people always face opposition from conservatives, and they must endure the loneliness and isolation of the misunderstood. They need courage.

They need tenacity. They need to have faith in their endeavor that isn't swayed by petty consideration of gain or loss. (DOY 2, ch. 16)

CULTURE

The wonderful art of peace is devoting ourselves entirely to linking beautiful human hearts with one another. When cultivated lives and culture itself are joined, the truly humane culture of the twenty-first century will be born. When fully realized humanity and art come together, truly humane art will be born. It is your mission to forge that spectacular and creative future. (DOY 2, ch. 16)

Peace and culture are one. A genuinely cultured nation is a peaceful nation, and vice versa. When conflicts multiply, culture wanes and nations fall into hellish existences. The history of the human race is a contest between culture and barbarity. As we leave the tensions of the Cold War behind, the pressing question becomes "What will the coming century be like?" Only culture is a force strong enough to end conflict and lead humanity in the direction of peace. (DOY 2, ch. 16)

The power of culture may be hard to detect at times, but it is a fundamental force since it transforms the human heart. Political and economic developments may be flashier and appear on the news more often, but culture and education are the forces that actually shape the age. We must not make the mistake of looking only at shallow waters that bubble noisily over the rocks; the deep currents are even more important to know the true nature of the river. (DOY 2, ch. 16)

A society that values culture is a society that values human happiness. President Makiguchi said that happiness lies in the pursuit of beauty, benefit and virtue. Benefit is the pursuit of all that is rewarding, in the broadest sense. Virtue is the pursuit of justice and opposition to injustice. Beauty is the pursuit of art and culture. All three of these pursuits contribute to our happiness. (DOY 2, ch. 16)

The Buddhist concept of cherry, plum, peach and damson—that each person should live earnestly, true to his or her unique individuality—has much in common with culture. Culture is the flowering of each individual's true humanity, which is why it transcends national boundaries, time periods and all other distinctions. Likewise, correct Buddhist practice means cultivating oneself and serving as an inspiration for others to lead truly cultured lives. (DOY 2, ch. 16)

American philosopher and educator John Dewey (1859–1952) said: "Genuine culture stimulates the creative powers of imagination, of mind and of thought. It includes not merely free access to things of mind and taste already in existence, but a positive production of them, so that the waters of knowledge and of ideas are kept really fresh and vital." Culture is a stimulus. Culture is to produce things of value. Culture enriches life. Culture belongs to the people. (6/15/96)

The English words *culture* and *cultivate* share the same linguistic root. Buddhist practice is also an undertaking to cultivate our inner life and spirit. In that sense, Buddhism and culture are intrinsically related. As members of the SGI, let us continue to vigorously carry out our great cultural movement in the pursuit of cultivating "fertile plains of peace" and "flower gardens of friendship" for the benefit and prosperity of all humanity. (6/23/96)

DEMOCRACY

When viewed over the short-term, Gandhi's advocacy of nonviolent resistance to the Nazis might seem idealistic to the point of being unrealistic. From the longer perspective, looking back over the history of the postwar period, I think that we must acknowledge the truth of this "voice in the wilderness"—the truth that he continued to assert even during war—that nonviolence represents the only means by which true liberty and democracy are realized. The mistrust and pessimism that beset our age make even more urgent the need for Gandhi's brand of optimism, for his kind of proudly declared faith in humanity. (2/11/92)

Nichiren Daishonin's Buddhism is the great Law that enables all people to develop their inherent Buddha nature and attain Buddhahood. It is the supreme teaching, which elucidates individual freedom and equality and the dignity of life in a logical and realistic manner, enabling people to bring out these qualities in their daily lives and in society. This is what prompts Nichijun Shonin, the sixty-fifth high priest, to state unequivocally that the Daishonin's Buddhism is the world religion that will form the foundation for realizing true democracy. He also points out that "irrational teachings" keep the people in ignorance, obstruct the development of individual potential and are enemies to democracy. (9/23/91)

Obviously, it is essential that people awaken and develop strength and discerning powers of criticism and judgment. My mentor, President Toda, encouraged us to remain engaged in public affairs, and this is the basis for our ongoing grass-roots endeavors to raise people's awareness. (1999 PP)

In society, it is vital that people develop solid characters and possess sound judgment, wisdom and clear values so as to be able to monitor and check developments in all spheres of society, including economics and government affairs, to lead society forward. They must have the ability to keenly discern the meaning behind various movements and whether leaders are truly working in the interests of the people. Based on the principle of the inner transformation of human life, the SGI movement is creating a fundamental path of stability, progress and humanism throughout the world toward the twenty-first century. (Dialogue 1, 1994)

Quite simply, there can be no true democracy unless the citizens of a country realize that they are sovereign, that they are the main protagonists, and then with wisdom and a strong sense of responsibility take action based on that realization. Democracy cannot be successful in its mission unless the people rouse themselves to become more informed and involved, unless they unite, unless they establish an unshakable force for justice and keep a strict eye on the activities of the powerful. (5/26/98)

Discussing all things openly as siblings or members of a family, please proceed hand in hand, step by step, toward construction and growth. In this sense, the world of Buddhism must be a model of democracy. (2/19/90)

When citizens lose the vibrant desire to "cause something to happen" for the betterment of their society, democracy is reduced to an empty shell. As members of the SGI, a movement that fosters peace, culture and education, we, too, are always trying to make things happen. That is what makes us strong and why we are never defeated. (2/25/96)

DISARMAMENT

I have repeatedly stressed that nuclear arms mean catastrophe for all humankind and that we must transcend national boundaries in combating them, working together not for the benefit of individual national interests but for the benefit of humankind, not for national sovereignty but for the sovereignty of the human race. The problem is how to shift the importance of national sovereignty from an absolute to a relative concern. (1990 PP)

Another problem that stands out against the backdrop of the many conflicts found throughout the world is the issue of arms exports. Many weapons, which have actually served to exacerbate regional conflicts, have been sold by countries with permanent seats on the U.N. Security Council. We have reached the point where it is essential that restrictions be imposed on the international arms trade and greater efforts made to strengthen the movement toward disarmament. (1993 PP)

～

The abolition of nuclear weapons is more than a question of their physical riddance. Even if all nuclear arsenals are depleted, a serious question will remain as to how to deal with the knowledge of nuclear arms production acquired by humankind. This is why I say that the only real solution to the issue of nuclear arms is to struggle incessantly against that "evil of life" that threatens the survival of humanity. (1997 PP)

EDUCATION

Shakyamuni waged a head-on struggle against dogmas that enchain and divide human beings. He strictly admonished, "The one who is full of rigid, fixed views, puffed up with pride and arrogance, who deems himself 'perfect,' becomes anointed in his own opinion because he holds firmly to his own views." Shakyamuni, who believed in continually seeking self-improvement, plunged into the realities of society as an "educator" in pursuit of a truly humane way of life, not as an absolute being who looked down on the people. (9/22/93)

～

The level of culture that teachers themselves have attained in the depths of their lives through their own personal efforts is conveyed from one human being to another, from teacher to pupil. Education is not something that is conferred in a high-handed manner from without. Consequently, teachers' inner growth contributes to the pupils' happiness and both educational and social advances. (9/27/91)

Victor Hugo wrote that those who open schools close down the prisons. This is his way of expressing symbolically the significance of education. The opening of schools sheds the light of humanity on society and does away with the need for prisons, which symbolize darkness. (9/27/91)

The French philosopher Charles Péguy asserted that a crisis in civilization and society is indicative of a crisis in education. Civilization is placed in jeopardy when humanity is jeopardized or crushed by political force or religious authority. Since teachers are the representatives of humanism, education provides the key to overcoming crises in this area. As a result, protecting education is protecting civilization; transforming education, meanwhile, serves to transform society. Indeed, the extent to which humanistic education flourishes is the barometer of civilization. (9/27/91)

It is my belief that education, in the broadest sense of the word, holds the key to meeting the challenges of global responsibility and fostering tolerance. Education does not mean coercing people to fit one rigid and unvaried mold; this is merely ideological indoctrination. Rather, true education represents the most effective means of fostering the positive potential inherent in all people: self-restraint, empathy for others and the unique personality and character of each person. To do this, education must be a personal, even spiritual encounter and interaction between human beings, between teacher and learner. (1998 PP)

Mr. Makiguchi, our mentor, once said: "Teachers must not instruct students with the arrogant attitude of 'Become like me!' It is far more important for teachers to adopt the attitude: 'Don't satisfy yourself with trying to become like me. Make your model someone of higher caliber.'" True teachers [who are genuinely concerned for the development of each student], therefore, are those who have the humility to advance together with their students. (1/27/93)

Education must never be coercive. The heart of education exists in the process of teacher and pupil learning together, the teacher drawing forth the pupil's potential and raising the pupil to eventually surpass the teacher in ability. (1/27/93)

Reading literature can greatly enhance the study of science. If science is all one focuses on, the mind will grow very mechanical. We are only fully human when we possess not only intelligence but also emotion and sensitivity. Literature is the oil that greases the wheels of the mind. (DOY 2, ch. 18)

The greatest enemy of learning is fear. This is true of language, of art, of every area of study. When we're afraid of being laughed at, of embarrassment, of being looked down on by others for our mistakes, shortcomings or limitations progress becomes very difficult. We must be brave. So what if others laugh? Whoever makes fun of those trying their best are the ones who should be ashamed. (DOY 2, ch. 16)

Mr. Makiguchi taught that education is the highest of all arts, the art of creating the value of fine character. His words are golden. Art does not belong to a select few. Nurturing people, cultivating the self, is also an art. Art is displayed in a beautiful life, beautiful actions, beautiful prayer. (DOY 2, ch. 16)

ENVIRONMENTAL ISSUES

The Universal Declaration of Human Rights is the crystallization of the wish to guarantee human existence for all people based on the resolve not to repeat the tragedies of World War II. Likewise, the Earth Charter should be a distillation of the spirit of coexistence and the resolve not to pass down the evils perpetrated by modern civilization to subsequent generations. Realization of such a charter will certainly involve many difficulties, but we have no choice but to forge the path toward it by sharing responsibility for our common struggle against global crisis and by building trust through sustained dialogue. (1997 PP)

Indeed, the threat to human life today consists not only of war or nuclear holocaust but also of the destruction and deterioration of the Earth's environment. Protection of the global environment must be made one of the top priorities of international politics, and the whole issue of national security should be reappraised, incorporating environmental concerns. (1991 PP)

The essence of our environmental problem is how we can go about creating a society that will exist in harmony with the ecosystem. For this reason, it is a compound problem that transcends the boundaries of politics, economics, science and technology. The environmental issue concerns fundamental problems of how human beings live and includes all fields of endeavor, which range from human values to the nature of culture in future societies. This is an issue that cannot be solved successfully from only the political or economic viewpoint of individual nations. We must instead proceed with a reformation of the consciousness of all the Earth's people, a task that renders the need for internal spirituality all the more necessary. (1992 PP)

The universe itself has imparted to humanity the mission of protecting the complex ecological system and of contributing to the creation of value within the Earth's biosphere. Consequently, if a sense of this lofty mission orients all of our scientific technology, social systems, politics and economics, we will discover the truly humane—in the best sense of the word—approach to solving environmental problems. (9/90 ST)

Bodhisattvas live for the sake of the future, which they strive to understand ahead of time through compassion and wisdom. They work to amplify the creative vitality of Earth's biosphere and to make full use of scientific technology and social systems for the sake of our children and for still unborn emissaries of the universal life force. (9/90 ST)

Enabling the masses to expand their awareness to the global level is of the utmost importance. Furthermore, this revolution of understanding and approach must be allowed to penetrate to the deepest layers of consciousness where it can influence judgments and actions in daily life. Each individual is concerned about the state of the air in their immediate vicinity. The problem is for each individual to be equally as concerned about pollution of the air everywhere. We must learn to control our own material desires (greed) for the sake of the good of people who live decades or even centuries after us. We must sacrifice convenience in the name of energy conservation. The question is whether we can change our lifestyles to the extent necessary to achieve this great goal. (9/90 ST)

Government must be dedicated to the good of the people. It is a tragedy that the beautiful natural environment people have cherished and protected for generations is being destroyed in the name of economic growth, political advantage and scientific progress. Because human beings have the capacity to be aware of the balance of nature, it is our duty to work to preserve it. (DOY 2, ch. 17)

I always press my camera's shutter with the desire to engage in a dialogue with nature. Through that dialogue, I see my true self—I see a true image of humanity and life. Nature is like a mirror. It remains still, but I move. It seems unchanging, yet I am constantly changing. The mirror of nature reflects my inner world, the essence of humanity, and the great, all-embracing expanse of life itself. (DOY 2, ch. 16)

The question is will we allow ourselves to be dragged down to the lower states of life or will we advance to the higher states? Only intelligence, culture and religious faith can lead us out of the Animality that thoughtlessly consumes nature, leaving a barren wasteland. Because of the oneness of life and its environment, a barren, destructive mind produces a barren, devastated natural environment. The desertification of our planet is created by the desertification of the human spirit. (DOY 2, ch. 16)

We all want to be healthy. For that reason, we want to breathe clean air, to see beautiful flowers and greenery. We turn to nature for this, just as a sunflower turns to the sun. We must recognize that any action transgressing or negating nature is a terrible mistake. All the money in the world won't buy the blue sky. The sun and the breeze belong to everyone. Human beings can either destroy nature or live in harmony with it. We must never forget that we are only a part of nature. (DOY 2, ch. 16)

~

Life is a chain. All things are related. When any link is harmed, the other links are affected. We should think of the environment as our mother—Mother Soil, Mother Sea, Mother Earth. There is no crime worse than harming one's mother. (DOY 2, ch. 16)

~

We are dependent on the Earth, not the other way around. In our arrogance, we have flagrantly overlooked this. The Soviet cosmonaut Yuri Gagarin (1934–68), the first person to see the Earth from space, declared it a blue planet. The blue of the oceans, the white of the clouds—they are proof that Earth is the water planet, a planet sparkling with life. The essential teaching of Buddhism is that the life of the Buddha resides in every plant and tree, even in the smallest dust mote. No philosophy has more profound reverence for life. (DOY 2, ch. 16)

~

One who loves nature can cherish other humans, value peace and possess a richness of character unfettered by selfish calculations of personal gain or loss. Those who live in a calculating way will end up calculating their own worth detrimentally. Such a life is limited in the extreme. Nature, however, is infinite. Though it may seem beneficial to keep track of personal gain or loss, from nature's broader viewpoint, this is actually a poor, miserable existence. Such people only hurt themselves. (DOY 2, ch. 16)

GLOBALIZATION

While it cannot be denied that nationality or ethnicity is a prime point to which we turn in establishing our identity, there is little prospect that nationalism in itself will lead to the formation of a new global order. The late Norman Cousins, who was my friend, asserted that the primary mission of education lies in teaching people not to be "tribe-conscious" but to be "human-conscious" in their thinking. In other words, tribalism, or nationalism, which remains in all of us at some subconscious level, must be cultivated and elevated by means of education, philosophy and religion to a more open and universal consciousness directed toward humanity as a whole. Without this fresh consciousness, a new world order will never materialize. (1/30/91)

I believe that cultural uniqueness is in no way incompatible with universality. Cultures that are rich in distinctiveness and originality stir people's minds and hearts everywhere; it is these cultures that move us by their pervasive universality. Indeed, this is why culture has historically spread freely, transcending the barriers of race and nation. (1989 PP)

In an increasingly internationalized world, it is no longer productive or meaningful merely to stress the tenacity of racial and national identity or its uniqueness. To continue to do so would plunge the world into chaos. The Pax Russo-Americana, although sustained by enormous quantities of destructive power, did represent a kind of order, and its disintegration does indeed threaten to revive the specter of nationalism all over the world. This must be avoided at all cost.... The gravity of the problem of nationalism makes all the more pressing the need to overcome it. However difficult the task may be, the establishment of principles and ideals that are at once universal in orientation and global in scope is an inescapable necessity if we are to cope successfully with the challenges of the coming century. (1989 PP)

The building of a world community, a global civilization of justice, compassion and hope must begin by turning away from the "eat or be eaten" ethos of competition, cultivating in its place a shared ethos of cooperation and interdependence which is in fact closer to the original sense of the word *competition*. In this regard, I would like to propose the concept of shared or mutual value-creation as a tenet for the new era. (1998 PP)

As we enter the new century, several problems demand our most urgent attention. In particular, economic globalization today proceeds at a furious pace. We must have the vision to orient this in such a way as to contribute to the creation of a truly rich and diverse age—toward a global civilization. (1999 PP)

HISTORY

The study of history is the study of humanity. Although not everyone can be a professional historian, it is important to use history as a mirror to guide us in shaping the future. You are

the protagonists who will write a fresh history of humanity.
(DOY 2, ch. 14)

∼

Without a mirror, it's impossible for you to see your own face
or full appearance. Similarly, armed with the mirror of history, you can see what needs to be done in the present. (DOY
2, ch. 14)

∼

Mr. Toda stressed the importance of history. He said history is
a signpost to help us move with greater certainty from past to
present, from present to future, toward the goals of peace and
the harmonious coexistence of all humankind. (DOY 2,
ch. 14)

∼

History in books is full of errors. But one's own history, the
history written only in one's heart, cannot record a single
falsehood or embellish anything. (DOY 2, ch. 14)

∼

The only way to achieve a sense of history is to study many
things, think about many things, and experience many things.
It is crucial to remain objective. You must always seek the
facts, the truth, without succumbing to personal bias or self-
interest. Never accept a lie. (DOY 2, ch. 14)

∼

It is important to study the lessons of history. Take the Holocaust, for example. Why did the mass murder of 6 million
Jews by the Nazis take place? How could such a tragedy have
occurred in a modern society in the twentieth century, in the
modern state of Germany? These are not, of course, simple
questions. They must be considered from many different

perspectives, and they are questions that human beings must continue to ask themselves eternally. (Dialogue 11, 1994)

Young people are the leaders of the twenty-first century. For that reason it is important that you have an understanding of history, that you can see through to the heart of things. A penetrating view of history is essential. A superficial one won't suffice. (5/26/98)

HUMAN RIGHTS

Alongside the need for an improved institutional framework, there must be a parallel effort to create a robust culture of human rights. Simply put, this means cultivating the awareness that human rights are not something special but norms of behavior that should be accepted and adhered to everywhere. While such an effort will take time, in the end it will be the most effective way of closing the gap between the ideal of human rights and reality. (1998 PP)

At every opportunity, I have asserted that Buddhism thoroughly protects the sanctity of life and the freedom of the human spirit, and that this constitutes our mission. At times such as these, however, when a crisis is once again building, I wish to take the further step of reaffirming, as part of our religious belief, that we will go to all lengths to uphold the sanctity of life, the freedom of the human spirit, and genuine democracy. We are naturally committed to protecting the freedom of religious belief. Furthermore, responding to any crisis of human dignity that may emerge, we must be prepared to protect people whose rights are in danger, or who are threatened by tyranny or oppression, even if their beliefs and opinions differ from our own. For example, we should protect people who practice different religious faiths, as well as people who uphold systems of thought that deny religion altogether, because this is a necessary outgrowth of the core tenets of Buddhism, which extol equally the dignity of humanity. (1996 PP)

When seeking to define human rights in the broadest sense, I believe that the right to live in a truly humane way can be said to constitute the essence of human security. Human rights are fundamental and must take priority over all else; without human rights, neither peace nor human happiness is possible. Because human rights represent the most sublime and inalienable value, endowing people with their distinctly human character, their violation cannot be permitted, whether by states or by any other force. (1996 PP)

I wish to declare that the struggle to defend the sanctity of life must never be aimed only at "secular security"—what I have called "the revolution of external forms alone." To make outward reforms thorough and genuine, I believe it is crucial that we turn our eyes inward, toward our inner selves. Legal and institutional guarantees of "freedom" and "democracy" as well as "peace" and "human rights" are indispensable, but they alone are not enough to preserve human dignity. (1997 PP)

Buddhism stresses the quality of our motivation, valuing that which issues spontaneously from within, as expressed in the simple phrase "Our heart is what matters most." It teaches that the ultimate objective of Shakyamuni's life was revealed in the humanity he manifested in his behavior and actions. Thus the cultivation and perfection of a person's character is considered in the Buddhist tradition to be the true goal of religious training. Norms that are not inner-generated and do not encourage the development of individual character are ultimately weak and ineffective. Only when external norms and inner values function in a mutually supportive manner can they enable people to resist evil and live as genuine advocates and champions of human rights. (1998 PP)

Everyone has a right to flower, to reveal his or her full potential as a human being, to fulfill his or her mission in this world. You have this right, and so does everyone else. To scorn and violate people's human rights destroys the natural order of things. We must become people who prize human rights and respect others. (DOY 2, ch. 1)

Buddhism places the highest value on human rights and seeks to ensure that human rights are respected. In caring for just one person, one tries to thoroughly protect and do everything he can for that person. One who respects and embraces the children of the Buddha in this way is a truly capable person and a true leader. (2/21/90)

Dr. Martin Luther King Jr., a tireless crusader for human rights, said: "Life's most persistent and urgent question is, What are you doing for others?" Do not say you will do it "someday"; now is the time. Do not say "someone" will do it; you are the one. Now is the time for youth to take full responsibility and courageously pave the way for the people's triumph. (8/18/96)

The innate power of humanity is the driving force that breaks down all barriers of discrimination. The ultimate expression of this humanity is Buddhahood; it is the power of the Mystic Law. Daimoku is therefore the fundamental energy for realizing victory in the struggle for human rights. (1/6/96)

~

We have to raise people's awareness of human rights through education. Our schools must teach human rights, our religions must teach human rights, and our government must respect human rights. (DOY 2, ch. 12)

~

Unless we can build a society that regards human beings not as a means to a goal but as the goal itself, we will remain forever a society of discrimination, unhappiness and inequality in a world of Animality, where the strong prey upon the weak. We will simply repeat the same abusive patterns. (DOY 2, ch. 12)

~

To study human rights, we must study philosophy. We must study Buddhism. And just as important as studying philosophy is the willingness to stand up for our beliefs and to take action. Human rights will never be won unless we speak out, unless we fight to secure them. (DOY 2, ch. 12)

~

The Soka Gakkai's movement is a human rights struggle by the people, for the people. Our movement's history is one of extending a helping hand to those suffering, lost and forgotten. To people exhausted by sickness and poverty; people devastated by destructive relationships; people alienated and forlorn as a result of family discord or broken homes, we have shared people's sufferings and risen together with them. (DOY 2, ch. 12)

~

Human rights, democracy and peace are a single entity. When one disintegrates, they all disintegrate. Leaders in all spheres of society must engrave this truth in their minds. (DOY 2, ch. 12)

~

In a society where there is no fundamental respect for human rights, reputation and standing are nothing. The most important thing is whether we have genuine love and compassion for others. (DOY 2, ch. 12)

~

Our every effort must be for people. Everything depends on people. Human rights are the distillation of these essential truths. (DOY 2, ch. 12)

~

Every sphere of human endeavor in education, culture, science, government, business and economics will either guarantee and foster human rights or come to a dead end. In education, for example, schools should exist for the sake of the students. Yet today it is as if the students exist for the sake of the schools. (DOY 2, ch. 12)

~

Having your rights as a human recognized by others is not just having people behave sympathetically toward you. Be proud of yourself as an individual, regardless of your disability. You must be proud of your mission. Those who laugh at you and make fun of you are cruel and wrong. They create a terrible burden of negative karma for themselves by ignoring your right to be treated as a human being. Letting their taunts get to you is a defeat for human rights. Your strength, however, is a victory for human rights. (DOY 2, ch. 12)

We need to refocus on the importance of benefiting humanity and make a fresh departure from there. This is how human rights will be established. (DOY 2, ch. 12)

We must make the twenty-first century a century of human rights. We must build a society with more than short-term profit as its goal. To do that, the first step is respecting ourselves, living with dignity, self-confidence and pride. Such people can then treat others with respect. (DOY 2, ch. 12)

A great river begins with a tiny drop of water and, from that humble beginning, flows into the sea. The current toward a century of human rights has just begun. (DOY 2, ch. 12)

One of the first steps in achieving human rights is appreciating and embracing individuality. It's also important to develop a solid perspective about humanity, realizing that though others may be different from you, we are all members of the same human family. (DOY 2, ch. 12)

Human rights are the sun illuminating the world. So, too, are love of humanity, kindness and consideration. All these things light our world. Their light brings cherry, plum, peach and damson into glorious bloom in society, enabling everyone to reveal their unique potential. (DOY 2, ch. 12)

Your mission is to make the sun of human rights rise on the twenty-first century. To do that, you must make the courageous sun of love for humanity rise first in your own hearts. (DOY 2, ch. 12)

Humanity

It is not simply strength in numbers that overthrows oppressors, but the strength of the human spirit—the strength of the spiritual solidarity of the people. Vaclav Havel, president of Czechoslovakia, is a farsighted leader who knows this well. A Czechoslovak acquaintance once remarked: "We in Czechoslovakia viewed communism as something fixed and immovable like the Himalayas. Then, in an instant it fell away." (Dialogue 7, 1994)

≈

To quote the great French social anthropologist Claude Levi-Strauss: "Tolerance is not a contemplative position dispensing indulgence to what was and what is." It is wrong to be tolerant of evil perpetrated by those in power. True tolerance is the dynamic approach of forging open relations with all people—to stand on the side of humanity and the people, and there wage a resolute struggle by nonviolent means; to spread the force of good through dialogue. (Dialogue 13, 1994)

Literature

To build a humanistic society where people live with dignity, we must have leaders acquainted with great literature. This is extremely important. (DOY 2, ch. 13)

≈

Literature is the study of humanity. It is the study of oneself and of the infinite realm of the human heart. Without an understanding of people's hearts, one cannot gain a profound understanding of any other sphere of learning or endeavor. Human culture is a product of the human heart and mind. (DOY 2, ch. 18)

~

If national leaders know nothing but science, it may well be that they will think only of building weapons. A knowledge of great literature breathes life into our humanity. Literature derives from the human spirit. (DOY 2, ch. 18)

~

Literature is the very pulse of life. Those who have learned to appreciate great literature during their youth are always vital and vigorous, because the pulse of literature beats in them. Those who haven't learned such appreciation lack that vitality; their lives are spiritually drab and empty. (DOY 2, ch. 18)

~

Actually, dividing things into humanities and sciences is itself odd. As long as so many political leaders and educators remain caught up in their specialties, unaware of the vital importance of literature, we will never create a better society. It will be very dangerous if our society is made up of people who, like robots, possess knowledge but no heart or conscience. (DOY 2, ch. 18)

~

Beautiful poetry isn't a bunch of fancy words and phrases. True beauty only comes from a beautiful spirit. I believe, too, that beautiful words come from a spirit that fights for humanity amid life's vicissitudes. Poetry is the product of trying to express in words the emotion we feel in everyday life. So is literature. (DOY 2, ch. 18)

❧

All great literature, ancient and modern, is a bridge connecting one human being to another, one spirit to another. The quality of our lives is determined by how many of these bridges we cross. (DOY 2, ch. 18)

NUCLEAR WEAPONS

With the invention of nuclear arms, war as a nation's sovereign right became an act that could lead directly to the annihilation of the human race. Because of that, as I have repeatedly stressed, humankind has no choice but to learn to transcend the framework of the state, to master the shift in perceptions from "national" to "human" interests, from the sovereignty of the state to the sovereignty of humanity. The question always in my mind, therefore, is how our system can be transformed into one built on the idea of human sovereignty. (1991 PP)

❧

The end of the Cold War has rendered the idea of nuclear deterrence meaningless, and I believe this is precisely the time we should pursue the total abolition of nuclear weaponry. (1994 PP)

ROLE OF RELIGION

The original purpose of religion is to serve humanity and to lead people to happiness. Toward this end, the Daishonin's Buddhism is the ultimate Law that champions humanity and

delivers freedom and dignity equally to all human beings, refusing to bend to authoritarian power or force. (9/23/91)

Even as we pursue the ideal of cultural pluralism, we cannot
overlook the existence of those values that are truly universal
and which must be protected against the encroachments of
relativism. These are not, however, externally imposed norms
but values that reside in, and are inherent to, the lives of all
people. Religious faith can provide the impetus for the clar-
ification and strengthening of such values, and the capacity to
do this is, in my view, the most essential criterion for any future world religion. (1998 PP)

The public space—the citizens' field of endeavor—is an in-
termediate zone between government and the private sec-
tor. But in the sterile atmosphere of contemporary urban
society developing this kind of vital linguistic space is extremely difficult. This kind of linguistic space is the cradle of
world citizens. Generating this space is the foremost task of
religion, especially of a world religion that would provide
the core ethos for the twenty-first century. I believe that religion, when it promotes unremunerated action, represents
the essence of public volunteerism. For this kind of religion
provides meaning, motivation and a solid framework for social action. (1999 PP)

Part of the mission of a religious organization like ours is to
provide a place of shelter, healing and comfort for the weary.
But that is not all. Religion should also help people discover
themselves anew, find liberation, reform their consciousness
and elevate their souls. Fulfilling these functions constitutes
the real worth of religion in relation to reforming the times.

Only then can it contribute to overcoming the identity crises and bridge the gap between local concerns and the overarching goals of global civilization. (1999 PP)

Religion is the stronghold, the final bastion, of the people's spiritual freedom and independence. If this last bastion falls, the imbalance of power will run rampant throughout all areas of human activity, making for an oppressive society. This problem affects everyone. (Dialogue 4, 1994)

A half-century ago, Mr. Makiguchi spoke out against "the crime of a ruling class ignorant of religion." The people then in power insisted that strong religious faith was important, but it was wrong to have exclusive faith in one school or denomination, and they suppressed any religion that was self-assertive and tried to have an identity of its own. We must not forget this history nor allow it to be repeated. (Dialogue 13, 1994)

The religious and spiritual challenge presented by a strong religious establishment independent of the government serves as a bastion of freedom against government control over the people's spiritual realm. A religious revolution staged by the people will be inextricably linked to political and other types of social revolution. With a living religion, this is always the case. (Dialogue 13, 1994)

In shaping political destiny, ethical and moral values based on religion play a large and important role. If religion is banished from daily life, it becomes impossible to make any spiritual contribution to society's development. (Dialogue 8, 1994)

Many criticized Gandhi, claiming that he was mixing religion with politics. But Gandhi replied to his critics by saying that politics bereft of religion is worthless, nothing but a lifeless system. Social or political movements without firm ideals and both spiritual and religious values are doomed to failure. (Dialogue 8, 1994)

Spiritual values are desperately needed. The Greek poet Euripides (c. 484–406 B.C.E.) wrote: "The reason that a single person of truth is stronger than a great multitude of those who are false is that the gods and justice are on the side of the true." (Dialogue 8, 1994)

Religious strife must be avoided at all cost; under no circumstance should it be allowed. People may hold different religious beliefs, but the bottom line is that we are all human beings. We all seek happiness and desire peace. Religion should bring people together. It should unite the potential for good in people's hearts toward benefiting society and humanity toward creating a better future. (2/12/98)

PEACE

Exchange between cultures, between countries, between human beings—this coming and going on what may be described as a new Silk Road may well go unnoticed or appear as only tiny ripples. Yet one ripple leads to another and yet another, until there are countless waves—waves that will hold afloat the ship of peace. By linking people's hearts, these waves will carry the world toward a greater atmosphere of friendship. It is our SGI movement that is creating the waves for that time. (6/2/92)

Chilean President Patricio Aylwin once said: "Respect for truth is fundamental to any form of coexistence.... Where there is no respect for truth, human trust disintegrates, giving rise to suspicion and a loss of credibility and causes people to succumb to hatred and the temptation to use force. Deceit is an antechamber to violence and is incompatible with peace." (4/11/92)

The way to peace, I believe, lies in extending and strengthening our international system, albeit in nascent and imperfect form, in the United Nations. To build such an order, we must foster public opinion in its support and establish the spiritual foundation or Zeitgeist that will permit it to function. It has been our consistent policy to support, in our capacity as a nongovernmental organization, the work and goals of the United Nations. (6/24/92)

The forces of divisiveness that tear at the human heart are the clear source of the crises imperiling humanity and all life, whether it be Earth's environment or dilemmas of nuclear and conventional weapons. Believing that divisiveness is inherently evil and unity is good, I have consistently argued that we can prevent the tragedies of human history from being repeated in the twenty-first century if we wield the power of good to allay divisive forces. This is my iron rule. (1997 PP)

Ways of resolving international problems and conflicts peacefully must be devised if we are to break successfully with the culture of war. Too often in the past, military intervention has been considered the only way. Although we cannot afford to overlook problems that pose a major threat to the international community, we must always be extremely cautious in opting for military force as a solution. In the final analysis, since force usually leaves scars that continue to fester, forcibly imposed hard power solutions are not real solutions at all. As Hegel suggested, no matter how much we try to justify or rationalize them, as long as the opponent regards them as unfair, such forceful measures will always lead to an intractable cycle of conflict and revenge. (1999 PP)

We must never lose sight of the fact that a third millennium imbued with respect for the sanctity of life, free from nuclear arms and war and rich with the rainbow hues of diversity, will come into being only through the efforts of empowered and responsible citizens who don't wait for someone else to take the initiative. (1998 PP)

Indeed, every one of us should realize that we possess the nobility of spirit to be the main actor in changing the course of history, and with that conviction, to undertake the task we share of solving the global issues of our time. We at the SGI, firmly committed to that conviction, will further expand our network of solidarity based on renewed humanism through our Buddhist-oriented movement fostering peace, culture and education. Working together with people of good throughout the world, we will rally courage and pool our wisdom to overcome the crises of civilization, now the greatest challenges humankind has ever faced, and open the door to a third millennium where the sanctity of each individual life shines with hope and glory. (1997 PP)

Although the third millennium will soon begin, this does not mean that a new era will come about naturally, without conscious effort. Such a renewal ultimately depends upon human will to open the door to a new age. Human beings have an innate ability to create new options and to make informed choices. The challenges before us may be difficult, but inasmuch as we ourselves have created them, it is clear that we also have the capability to resolve them. (1996 PP)

The coming twenty-first century begins the third millennium. We must not permit it to be stained with the same kind of brutality and bloodshed that has ravaged the present era. I strongly appeal to all people to prevent the spread of fanaticism, so often used to justify inhuman acts. The price we have had to pay has been enormous with every repetition of these tragedies. We must not let the painful lessons of the twentieth century go to waste; rather, we must overcome the divisive forces that have once again emerged and, in the little time remaining in this century, place the highest priority on generating the basis for a common struggle of humanity against global problems such as environmental degradation and poverty. (1996 PP)

The first goal of SGI members is to be good citizens of their own countries, and to contribute to the prosperity of their respective societies while showing proper regard for their own culture, customs and laws. The second is to work toward the realization of a permanent peace and to promote human culture and education on the basis of the Buddhist teachings of Nichiren Daishonin, which revolve around the sanctity of life. The third goal for SGI members is to reject war and all other forms of violence and to do everything possible to bring happiness to the human race and prosperity to the world. Two important ways to achieve this are to abolish nuclear weapons and realize a world free of war. Upholding the spirit of the U.N. Charter, members must cooperate in efforts to maintain world peace. (1995 PP)

The SGI's efforts are not limited to U.N.-centered endeavors for peace. We are also active in the spheres of culture and education as we strive to realize what we consider the social mission of religion. Our aim is to pursue humanism, to practice religion in the service of people and to take resolute action to overcome the immense problems now confronting humankind. (1996 PP)

In Mahayana Buddhism, which is the creed of the Soka Gakkai, there are ten potential conditions of life inherent in human beings, known as the ten worlds. According to this principle, people who start wars exist in the four lowest states of Hell, Hunger, Animality and Anger, known as the four evil paths. Controlled directly by instinct and desire, the thoughts and actions of those who start wars are inevitably foolish and barbaric. Therefore, from the Buddhist point of view, the issue of how to build the "defenses of peace" within the hearts of such individuals takes precedence over any external systemic factors and represents both the wellspring and the core of any attempt to build world peace. (1995 PP)

War has held humankind in its irrevocable grip throughout history; it is the source of all evil. War normalizes insanity—

insanity that does not hesitate to destroy human beings like so many insects, that tears all that is human and humane to shreds, producing an unending stream of refugees. War also cruelly damages our natural environment. As a Buddhist, I deeply believe that no individual can experience true happiness or tranquility until we turn humankind away from its obsession with war. We have already paid a heavy price for this lesson—that nothing is more tragic and cruel than war. I believe that our first priority is an obligation to our children to open a clear and reliable path to peace in the next century. (1995 PP)

Now that the twenty-first century is upon us, we must ask ourselves what kind of century we ultimately want it to be. Above all, we want it to be a century without war, in which people no longer take up arms against each other. To that end, we must begin to build a global cooperative system for peace. The greatest tragedy of the twentieth century has been the loss of human lives in war. Including civilians, it is estimated that 22 million people died in World War I and 60 million in World War II. One scholar called our era the "century of war dead." This folly must not be repeated in the third millennium. (1995 PP)

It is now time for us to put the bitter lessons of this century to good use and to ready ourselves for the leap forward into the third millennium. Now, more than ever, we require a vision backed by a solid philosophy, and we have to work to realize that vision through actions rooted in strong and dynamic optimism. We may draw courage from the words of French philosopher Alain (1868–1951), who observed, "Pessimism comes from our passions; optimism from the will." We must never abandon our confidence that, no matter what difficulties arise, humankind has the capacity to overcome them and to forge ahead. (1995 PP)

It is up to people themselves to build a world free from strife. The fate of the twenty-first century hinges on whether we give up the idea as impossible or continue to work at the difficult task of achieving true peace. According to archaeologists, humankind has engaged in organized war, meaning clashes between groups, for only about 10,000 of the 4 million years of human existence on earth. This fact should lead us to the conviction that it is not impossible to realize a human society in which war does not exist. (1994 PP)

In a world of growing interdependence among nations, it is no longer possible for any single country to flourish in isolation. We have no choice but to work together, searching for a road to peaceful coexistence and mutual prosperity. "Symbiosis," which means living and prospering together, has become the key word of our time, whether in reference to relationships among nations or between humankind and nature. What is needed now is a "total revolution for symbiosis," which can be achieved only through human revolution on a global scale. The SGI's movement for spiritual rebirth in the individual provides the foundation for these efforts. (1994 PP)

The main reason relations between different peoples and cultures degenerate into the kind of atrocity symbolized by "ethnic cleansing" is to be found in closed thinking and narrowness that grips people's minds. People of different ethnic groups who managed until only days before to live side by side without particularly overt problems are suddenly at each other's throats, as if prodded and moved only by hatred. It is difficult to believe that the recurrent strife and bloody conflicts we are witnessing today have broken out solely because the restraining frameworks of ideology and authoritarianism were removed. Economic hardship cannot explain it either, though it may have acted as the trigger; if that were the underlying cause, there would be no necessity to resort to killing. We can only conclude that the true cause lies deeper, in a disease of close-mindedness whose roots are submerged in the history of civilization. (1993 PP)

The Mystic Law, which forms the basis of our belief, is written with the Chinese character *myo*, which has three meanings: to "open," "be endowed," and "revive." As the first meaning suggests, the SGI is engaged in a Buddhist movement to open up the closed hearts and minds that are at the root of civilization's decline. We must all firmly commit ourselves to the historical endeavor of opening lines of dialogue and generating opportunities for openness and empathy among people everywhere—East and West, North and South. (1993 PP)

Shortly after the end of World War II, President Toda wrote in an article directed to the youth: "Our goal is to establish a base of eternal peace and security for all humanity. We must therefore be prepared to encounter oppression and persecution along the way. But if we give our lives for the sake of the Lotus Sutra, we will receive words of praise from Nichiren Daishonin when we arrive at Eagle Peak. What should we care, then, for trifling worldly honors in this lifetime! Young friends, stand up and join me in playing a full and active role in our endeavors!" (2/5/96)

Because of the oneness of life and its environment, a barren, destructive mind produces a barren, devastated natural environment. War is the most extreme example of this destructive impulse. War destroys both nature and the human spirit. This century has been a century of war and death. We must make the coming century a century of life and peace. We must make the twenty-first century one in which peaceful life is the top priority in all spheres of human activity—in commerce, in government, in science. (DOY 2, ch. 17)

WORLD CITIZENSHIP

It is of urgent necessity to educate as many people as possible to become "world citizens" in order to achieve everlasting peace. The curriculum should cover the most important themes humankind must grapple with today—the environment, development, peace, and human rights. Each one of these topics requires the new point of view of a world citizen, a perspective that goes beyond the confines of national entities. The above four themes are closely related to one another. The ultimate goal in studying them together is peace for the human race. (1988 PP)

It goes without saying that the existence of world citizens and national independence are not opposed to each other. In today's world it is fully possible to deepen one's own national and cultural identities and to take a broad look at the entire world while working for humanity. (1988 PP)

It has become clear that the solution to such global issues as the threat of nuclear warfare and environmental destruction require new approaches that transcend national boundaries.

Effective action to assure the survival of humanity cannot be taken as long as our thinking is bound within the narrow confines of the sovereign state. A way of thinking rooted firmly in a truly global outlook is the most pressing need of our times. (1989 PP)

When asked his nationality, Socrates is said to have replied that he was not only an Athenian but also a citizen of the world. His remark shows us the kind of philanthropic spirit that, transcending narrow bounds of nation, race and region, regards the whole world as its home. This attitude should be at the heart of world citizen education. (1987 PP)

In more concrete terms, the course of education for world citizens must encompass such currently vital problems as environment, development, peace and human rights. Education for peace should reveal the cruelty of war, emphasize the threat of nuclear weapons, and insist on the importance of arms reduction. Education for development must deal with the eradication of hunger and poverty and should devote attention to establishing a system of economic welfare for the approximately 500 million people who suffer from malnutrition today and to the two-thirds of the nations in the world that are impoverished. Harmony between humanity and the world of nature should be the theme of education in relation to the environment; it is vital to stimulate the most serious consideration to the extent to which nuclear explosions harm the ecosystem. Learning to respect the dignity of the individual must be the cornerstone of education in relation to human rights. In all four of these essential categories, education must go beyond national boundaries and seek values applicable to all humanity. Furthermore, to make possible the attainment of the paramount goal of peace for humankind, activities in all four areas must be conducted in a mutually interrelated fashion. In other words, world–citizen education must be inclusive, comprehensive education for peace. (1987 PP)

~

Friendship is the key. To never betray one's friendships, to nurture and develop strong, amicable ties—these are the qualities required of a world citizen. (DOY 1, ch. 9)

~

One of the necessary attributes of a world citizen is a shift in focus toward the welfare of humankind. Unless we discipline our spirits through our day-to-day experience, however, such a conceptual shift alone will not give us the strength we need to set a new course for our times. This is in fact one of the issues the SGI is now attempting to address through our movement for "human revolution." Simply stated, this movement is dedicated to encouraging people to become aware of their own boundless inner power and to take responsibility for the welfare of humankind. Although it may seem an indirect approach, I am convinced that this human revolution, with its principle of inner reformation first, is in fact the most certain path toward realizing a genuine global revolution. (1996 PP)

~

We can say with confidence that the most pressing need of our times is for world citizens who will respond with courage and imagination to the deepening global crisis of human dignity. (1996 PP)

~

Whether we can become good citizens of the world hinges upon the degree of self-control we achieve. It is, after all, the ability to see ourselves penetratingly that enables us to transcend national boundaries and ethnic barriers. Eternal peace is not a static condition but a continuum that is consciously maintained through the interaction of self-restraining individuals within a self-restraining society. Cooperation for peace is necessary in the areas of politics, economics, and education, of course. But the building of lasting peace depends on how many people capable of self-restraint can be fostered through religious guidance. If a religion is worthy of the name, and if it is one that can respond to the needs of contemporary times, it should be able to nurture in its followers the spiritual basis for becoming good citizens of the world. (1990 PP)

The goal of the SGI movement is nothing less than this: to instill an ethos of worldwide citizenry. By defining ourselves as citizens of the world, we will be able to revitalize the now nearly faded virtues of courage, self-control, devotion, justice, love and friendship and make them pulse vibrantly in people's hearts. (1994 PP)

While people are gradually beginning to acquire a global perspective, wars and struggles fought over racial, ethnic, and religious issues are as omnipresent as ever. By calling a Special Session on Education, the United Nations can effectively launch a campaign for educating world citizens that will encourage people to see that we are all passengers on one "spaceship Earth," that we are all members of the same "house." (1990 PP)

It is my hope and conviction that we will see a revival of philosophy—philosophy in the broadest, most Socratic sense of the term. Based on this kind of philosophy, an age of soft power will bear its truest, richest fruit. In a "borderless" age, such an internalized philosophy will serve as the mark and badge of world citizens. Those great standard-bearers of the American renaissance, for whose ideals I have enduring respect—Emerson, Thoreau and Whitman—were, I am convinced, world citizens of this caliber. (9/26/91)

As we aspire to realize a century of global unity, it is only natural that dialogues for peace and educational and cultural exchange that transcend the boundaries of religion, race and nationality will become ever more important. I believe the most productive approach is for each nation to compete with other in producing fine global citizens. In every society, competition, in the best sense, promotes progress. (5/17/94)

Founder of value-creating education and first Soka Gakkai president, Tsunesaburo Makiguchi (1871–1944), battled with Japanese militarism and died in prison at age 73. From the first years of this century, he insisted that the human race should no longer engage in military competition, political competition, or economic competition, but instead should aim for an age in which it competes on humanistic grounds. (5/17/94)

INDEX